how to grow
African Violets

BLOSSOM TYPES

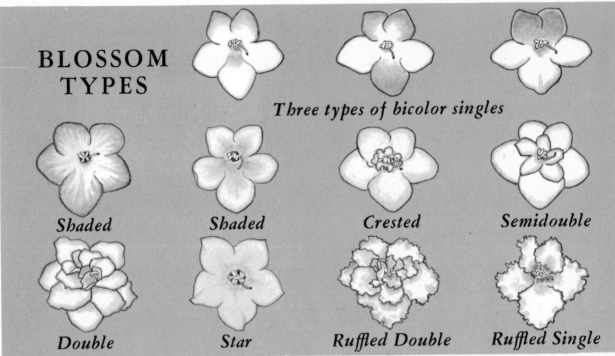

Three types of bicolor singles

Shaded   Shaded   Crested   Semidouble

Double   Star   Ruffled Double   Ruffled Single

LEAF TYPES

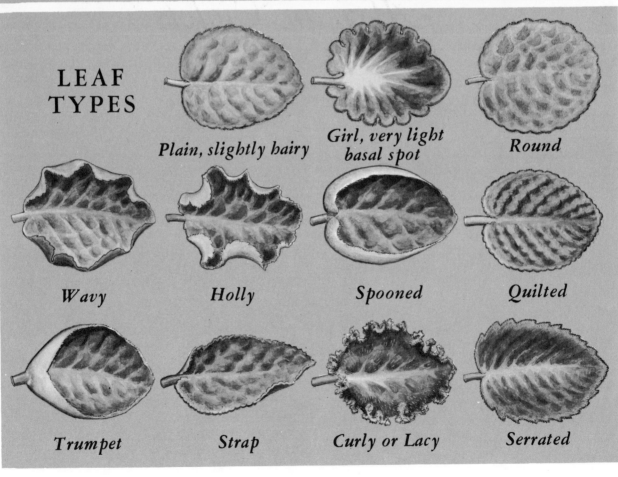

Plain, slightly hairy   Girl, very light basal spot   Round

Wavy   Holly   Spooned   Quilted

Trumpet   Strap   Curly or Lacy   Serrated

how to grow
African Violets

by Carolyn K. Rector

A Sunset Book

Lane Books • Menlo Park, California

ACKNOWLEDGMENTS

In preparation of this manuscript, the author gratefully acknowledges the help and encouragement given her by her friends Dorothy Behrends, the late Harvey Cox, Constance Hansen, Clarissa Harris, Inez Johnson, Genevieve Marsh, Hortense Mitchell, and Edna Whitlow. Special appreciation is also expressed to Mr. and Mrs. Hammond for supplying many of the photographs used in the revised edition and for checking artwork.

Cover photographs are from the collection of Sweeney, Krist and Dimm of Portland, Oregon. The variety pictured on the front cover is Lady Astor.

Library of Congress Catalog Card Number 62-12469

Title No. 305

Third Edition

Ninth Printing June 1970

Copyright © 1951, 1956, 1962

Lane Magazine & Book Company, Menlo Park, Calif.

Lithographed in U.S.A.

About This Book

When Mrs. Carolyn Rector first started growing African violets, very little was popularly known about their culture. In fact, the first plant she bought was sold to her as a "Santa Paula Violet" by a nurseryman who confessed he did not have the faintest idea how it should be cared for.

This first plant was a disappointment, for it stubbornly refused to bloom. Without a handy book to tell her how to overcome her plant's reluctance, Mrs. Rector had to piece together the information as best she could. She admits that she made all the mistakes that are expected of a beginner — and then some. By the time the plant finally flowered, she was fascinated and challenged by its culture. As she uncovered the answers to each new puzzle, she classified and assembled information in an orderly collection — and here it is.

Mrs. Rector hopes that her findings may help many beginners to fuller enjoyment of the African violet by saving them from making needless mistakes and suffering unnecessary disappointments. The expert saintpaulia fan may also find in this book some new idea to try in a potting mixture, a lighting set-up, or a quirk in pollinating.

With this new edition, Carolyn Rector's down-to-earth book celebrates its tenth anniversary. First published in 1951, it was so enthusiastically received that it was reprinted five times and republished in England by Blandford Press. A revised edition was issued in 1956 and it in turn passed through several printings. Now, because of the continuing demand for current information on African violet culture, Mrs. Rector has once again revised her popular book.

This new edition brings the reader up to date on cultural practices that have advanced since the book's last revision. It contains more drawings, a new chapter on Saintpaulia species, and additional detail scattered throughout.

Mrs. Rector is well known to hundreds of African violet fanciers throughout the world, with whom she maintains a voluminous correspondence. She was at one time president of the Los Angeles branch of the African Violet Society of America. She is the author of the master list of African violet varieties published by the national society. She has introduced many prize-winning, registered varieties, notably: Hermosa, Navarro, Silver Field, Silver Moon, Skywayman, Sunset Lane, Charm Song, Constancia, Even Song, Interlude, Moonhawk, Starsong, and Might Do.

Lois B. Hammond

AMERICA *used in arrangement*

Lois B. Hammond

WHITE GIRL *planted in hollowed-out rock*

Contents

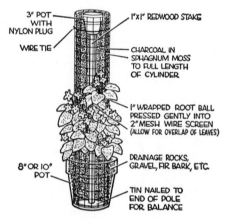

3" POT WITH NYLON PLUG

1"x1" REDWOOD STAKE

WIRE TIE

CHARCOAL IN SPHAGNUM MOSS TO FULL LENGTH OF CYLINDER

1" WRAPPED ROOT BALL PRESSED GENTLY INTO 2" MESH WIRE SCREEN (ALLOW FOR OVERLAP OF LEAVES)

8" OR 10" POT

DRAINAGE ROCKS, GRAVEL, FIR BARK, ETC.

TIN NAILED TO END OF POLE FOR BALANCE

Here is one way to display an entire collection in a small space. A 3-foot pole encased in wire forms frame for this column of African violets. Inside of pole, as diagrammed above, contains redwood stake that is surrounded by charcoal and sphagnum moss. Wash soil off violet roots, wrap in 1-inch ball of moss, and insert in hole poked in moss. Standard or semi-miniature varieties work best, keep in scale. Keep moist and feed once a month. Rotate pole daily.

CHAPTER ONE

The Number One House Plant

Not many years ago the first African violet hybrids were offered for general sale in this country by a nursery in Los Angeles. The newcomer had many appealing qualities that soon won it many friends. As the years passed, its circle of admirers widened and its friends increased in number, until today it is acknowledged to be the most popular house plant in the country.

The history of this lovely plant has been set down many times. Suffice it to tell that it was discovered in 1890 in its wild state in East Africa by Baron Walter von Saint Paul, for whom it was named "saintpaulia." Its popular name, "African violet," probably comes from its resemblance to the violet, although it is not related to this plant in any way. Baron von Saint Paul sent seeds to Europe, where plants were raised and exhibited in horticultural exhibits in 1893. The next year, seeds and plants were stocked by continental nurserymen, and two plants of the ionantha variety were imported by a nursery in New York. But the plant was practically unknown in this country until the 1920's, when the Los Angeles firm of Armacost & Royston, Inc., put on the market a quantity of saintpaulias grown from three leaves obtained from a local private estate. The firm carried on a program of cross-pollinating and created many new hybrids. At first, sales were modest, but by 1928 the firm had better than a half acre of African violets in cultivation under glass, and by 1933 it was selling thousands of plants a year. Soon afterward, Armacost & Royston turned their attention to orchids and roses, and by 1939 they were out of the African violet business altogether. But by that time, the plant had taken the popular fancy, and the great vogue for its culture was well under way.

The remarkable popularity of the African violet is easy to explain. It is an attractive plant, with handsome foliage and glowing blossoms, and with proper care, it will flower the year around. It is fairly easy to grow—although it has enough cranky traits to make its culture interesting.

The saintpaulia responds beautifully to thoughtful care. It seems to appreciate the attentions of an owner who gives it the proper amount of sunlight, ventilation, water, and plant food, and who keeps it clean, dusted and shorn of broken leaves and stems. It can also "turn" on the person who carelessly over-waters it, allows its leaves to burn in the direct sun, or fails to shield it from the waiting fungi, insects, and diseases that take over a poorly attended plant.

If you take its culture seriously, there are many things you can do with the African violet. You can readily propagate plants from leaf cuttings or from seed, or by dividing old plants. You can grow your own seed and experiment with breeding new varieties or sports. There is no apparent end to the range of potting soil mixtures and fertilizing programs that you can try for developing glossy foliage or richly colored blooms. If you produce an especially beautiful plant, you can enter it in one of the shows put on by the enthusiastic local branches of the African Violet Society of America.

Lois B. Hammond

LOVELY LADY

Lois B. Hammond

CINDERELLA'S SLIPPER

You should probably be warned of one restriction that may limit your activities. Some varieties of African violet are patented, and they cannot be propagated to be sold or given away without a license. If you plan to propagate such plants only to increase your personal collection, you can do so without a license. Patented plants are identified with a special tag, so you should have no difficulty in recognizing them at the nursery. Should you wish to propagate patented plants, you should write to the headquarters of the African Violet Society for information and addresses of the patent holders.

Interest in African violet culture often leads to fellowship with saintpaulia fanciers scattered over the country and throughout the world. Growers correspond with each other, exchanging cultural data through organized Round Robins. The magazines *Begonian* and *Flower Grower* have discontinued Round Robins, but if you become sufficiently engrossed in violet culture to share your ideas with other growers of African violets, you can write to me about these groups or for membership in one of them. The only Round Robins now circulating are some I am conducting. No fee is charged for joining a Round Robin.

CHAPTER TWO

How to Grow from Leaf Cuttings

Let us say that an African violet addict offers you a leaf from one of her prize plants. She tells you that all you have to do is set it in a glass of water on the kitchen window sill, and in no time at all you will have a fine plant, the first of what may turn out to be a houseful.

You will indeed find that starting plants from leaves is not a difficult thing to do, but you will also discover that there is more to the matter than simply abandoning the leaf to itself for a few months. There are some do's and don'ts that you should know about so you will not be disappointed.

You may start your leaf in either of two ways: you can start it in water or in a rooting medium such as sand.

Some varieties root very quickly, but most of the larger growing kinds, such as the Amazons, Supremes, and DuPonts are very slow. If your leaf seems to be taking its time about developing roots, do not be discouraged so long as it is plump and green and looks healthy.

Unless you have a reliable form of temperature control in your house, you will find that your leaves will root quicker and grow faster in the spring than at any other season. But with patience and a moderate amount of care, they can be grown at any time.

SELECTING LEAVES

If you are a dyed-in-the-wool African violet enthusiast, and someone offers you a leaf of a new or rare variety, you would accept it quickly, regardless of the age or size of the leaf. But if you are going to select a leaf to root, you would be more choosy.

In the first place, you would not pick out the largest leaf on the plant. The large leaves that grow in the bottom row are the oldest and, therefore, the first to die. They have almost lived out their span. They are usually very slow to take root, or they may give up entirely and simply rot. Nor would you pick out a small young leaf. Although young leaves may root very quickly, they are apt to produce small, delicate, slow-growing plants.

Preferably, you would select a medium-sized leaf that has not yet completed its full growth. It would be packed full of vigor and vitality, and will give you anywhere from one to a dozen husky young plants depending on the variety. Different varieties vary considerably in this respect. The large heavy types, such as the Supremes, Amazons, and DuPonts, usually send up only one or two sprouts, while some of the smaller-growing varieties may produce anywhere from six to a dozen.

If you receive some leaves by mail or otherwise, and they look limp and discouraged, examine them closely. If the end of the stem is still cleanly cut, or looks "healed," you will not need to cut off any more; but if it looks collapsed, cut the shriveled portion off with a sharp knife and let the stem dry for two or three hours. Immerse the entire leaf and stem in water to which a bit of vitamin B_1 has been added, and leave it there for a day or so. Often, this treatment will save even a badly wilted leaf.

CUTTING THE STEM

Some authorities recommend cutting the leaf stem very short, leaving about an inch or an inch and a half attached to the leaf, because a short stem roots quickly. However, short stems have disadvantages. If you start with a short stem and it rots instead of rooting, you have practically nothing left with which to work. But if you start with a fairly long stem and it begins to rot, you can cut it off well above the rotten spot and start all over again with the same leaf. Also, if you use a good length of stem, you may be able to get another crop from the stem by cutting it off when the first crop has grown large enough to live without the parent leaf.

If you split the stem about a half inch at the end, you will grow a bigger cluster of roots. Let the cut end dry for two or three hours before putting it in sand or water.

ROOTING IN WATER

Many a successful grower of African violets started out with a leaf in water. This is a very popular and fairly easy way to begin.

Secure a small amber or green glass bottle, such as those used for headache pills and vitamin tablets. In amber or green glass, violet stems will grow a better set of roots than they will in clear glass; and algae, or green scum, will not form so quickly.

Pour enough water into the bottle to cover the end of the stem about 1 inch. The reason for not filling the bottle to the top is that if the stem starts to rot it will rot under water first; and if only a small part of it is under water, the rot will be easier to detect and cut out before it affects the entire stem. If the stem is too short to reach the water, twist a bit of wicking around the stem, and let it hang down into the water. It will keep the stem wet enough to root.

Having placed your leaf in the bottle and put in the right amount of water, label the bottle with the name of the variety and the name of the person or firm from whom you received it. Use a wooden or plastic stick label, which you can fasten to the bottle with a rubber band and later transfer to a pot.

Stand the bottle in a warm place, away from draft. Place it in a good light but not the direct sun. The kitchen window sill is usually a good spot,

provided it does not receive strong sunlight. The glass bottle and the water inside will act like a burning glass when struck by the sun's rays and may cook the leaf.

Another popular method is to put several leaves in a glass to root. This method has one disadvantage over rooting in a flat-sided bottle: without the wall of the bottle to restrain them, the stems often curl right up out of the water after a few days. If you want to try this method, pour an inch or two of water in a glass, then fit a piece of tough paper over the top like a cap, and tie it firmly in place. Punch a hole in the paper for each leaf, and put the stems down through the hole until they are in the water.

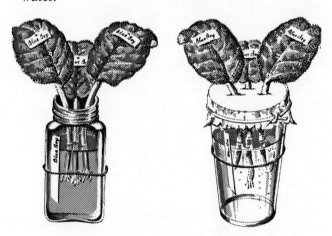

Two methods of rooting leaves in water

If you have more than one leaf in a bottle or glass, you will want to label each one separately. A good way is to write the variety name on a tiny piece of paper and stitch it to the leaf with a needle and thread. Place the slip of paper on the top side of the leaf, and tie the thread underneath.

Another very good way to mark leaves is to write the name on a very small piece of adhesive tape and stick this down on the upper side of the leaf. Always use ordinary lead pencil for marking, as indelible pencil or ink will blur if it gets wet.

Condition of Water

Ideally, the water used should be chemically pure. Although some growers successfully start

African violets in tap water, many people find their city water is too harsh for the delicate plants. If the water in your locality is very hard or contains much sulfur, this condition will interfere with the proper development of roots. As an alternative, you can use distilled water, obtainable from drug stores and filling stations. A quart will last quite a while for rooting leaves and starting seedlings. Or, you may use the water that melts off the frosted parts of your mechanical refrigerator when you defrost it. If you are starting your leaves in winter, you may save rain water or melted snow.

After you have started your leaves, do not change the water in the bottle or glass, but keep it at the same level by adding a little from time to time.

Some growers believe that a better set of roots will be produced if a nutrient solution is used instead of plain water. My experiments have not convinced me that this substitution has any noticeable effect on root growth, but if you want to try it, you can use any of the complete liquid fertilizers recommended for acid-loving plants. Be sure to dilute it so it is only about one-eighth as strong as the directions on the bottle recommend for growing plants. Do not use liquid manure at this stage.

One of my correspondents has a method which she thinks is the best yet. She puts the leaves in plain water for two weeks. After two weeks she changes to a nutrient solution of one quarter the strength used for plants. Two weeks later she changes again to a one-half strength solution. She reports that leaves will often root much faster with this treatment.

Many people prefer to leave the stems in the water until the tiny plants are forming at the base, because the plants will not take so long to appear above the surface of the planting medium after planting. But you will probably have better success by removing them from the water when the roots are a quarter of an inch to a half-inch in length.

First Potting

When the leaves are sufficiently rooted to be removed from the water, prepare enough 2-inch pots so that you will have a pot for each leaf. If the pots have been used before, they should be sterilized. Scrub them clean and boil them for a few minutes in a solution of one-half ounce of vinegar to 1 gallon of water. If they are new pots, soak them an hour or so in either a vinegar solution or in a solution containing household bleach, about as strong as you would use for bleaching clothes. Let them dry a little, then dip the rims in hot paraffin, melted in an old coffee can. Sealing the rim with wax prevents the stems from rotting where they lap over the damp earthenware. Another method, less bothersome and preferred by most people, is covering the rim with a strip of aluminum foil, crimped around the edge.

A very good treatment is to paint the rim of the pot, inside and out, with quick-drying shellac. If the pot is very rough in texture two coats are better than one.

There is also a type of adhesive tape, similar to masking tape, that many growers find practical for covering pot rims.

In the bottom of each pot place a 1-inch square of fine mesh plastic fly screen. Ram it down tightly. This keeps the dirt from washing through, and when the roots reach it they form a compact mass which comes out of the pot easily when it is time to divide and repot. If you cannot get screen, cover the drainage hole with a small piece of broken pot. The plastic screen is best, however, and it can be used over and over again.

Starting Medium

The starting medium should preferably be a neutral substance like sand, vermiculite (expanded mica), or puffed rock. It should not contain any kind of fertilizer and it should be sterile.

Plain sand, such as builders use for mixing concrete, makes a good medium, and it is easily obtained. Vermiculite is an excellent medium that is sold nearly everywhere. The puffed rock product, a white granular substance, is very popular. Algae or green moss grows very rapidly on the surface of this material if it is kept in the warm, light place that is best for violets, but this growth is harmless and will not interfere with your violet.

Before it is used, the starting medium should be sterilized to destroy fungus spores, weed seeds, and any pests that may be in it. Vermiculite and puffed rock are already sterile and require no treatment, but sand should be sterilized with boiling water. Put the sand in a sieve and pour boiling water through it three times. This will also wash out the dust and fine sand. Use the coarse-grained sand in preference to the fine.

You may want to experiment with other starting mediums. Some people successfully use a starting mixture containing leaf mold. Others have found leaf mold to encourage the growth of mildew and root rot, so you may not wish to risk a precious leaf in this mixture.

Another favored mixture is composed of equal parts of washed sand, vermiculite and Georgia peat (a slightly acid peat). This is a fine mixture for mature plants, but is probably a little too strong for starting leaves.

If you add peat or leaf mold to a starting medium, you should sterilize the mixture with boiling water or by one of the methods described in the chapter on potting soils.

If you have trouble with leaves rotting after the roots have started but before the leaf sprouts are up, try this method of preparing the rooting bed: put in first a half-inch layer of ground charcoal, dust and all; then add an inch of your rooting mixture and top it with a layer of vermiculite; and finally set the leaves in this.

Setting Rooted Leaves

There are three popular ways to set these rooted leaves in the first pot.

One way is to fill the pot to within an inch of the top with starting medium, lay the leaf on its side on top, and put a very thin coating of the mixture over the sprouting end. Of course, if the leaf is a bit heavy it will tip over, so peg it down either with toothpicks or a hairpin.

Another way is to fill the pot a little more than a third full, set the leaf in the pot, letting it lean against the side for support, and then put a thin layer of the mixture over the sprouting end.

Or you can fill the pot a little more than two-thirds full, set the leaf in it in an upright position, brace it with a stiff broomstraw down through the center of the leaf, and fill in about half an inch of soil. The straw will not do any harm to the leaf. If the leaf still does not want to stay in place, peg it down.

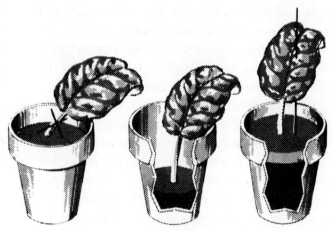

Three ways to set leaves in starting medium

Do not in any case put much covering over the stem tips. The deeper you plant the stems, the longer they will take to come up, and sometimes they seem to get discouraged and rot instead of growing. Keep them in a warm place, in a good light, but not in the sun. Keep them moist but not too wet. If you keep them too wet they may rot, but never let them get bone dry. *And always use warm water.*

Sometimes the stem will rot clear up to the leaf, or it may be accidentally broken off short. If the leaf is a very scarce variety, and you are anxious to save it, try standing it on edge, with the cut edge down, of course, in damp sand or vermiculite. Hold it in place with toothpicks. Do not set more than a quarter of an inch of the edge under the surface. For the first few days, cover the leaf with an inverted glass.

14

Many people think that in a case like this it is a good idea to cut away part of the leaf on each side to the central vein, thus making a stem for it. Use a razor blade for cutting, so that none of the leaf cells will be crushed. Let the leaf dry for several hours till the cut edges are dry; then plant as before described.

ROOTING IN A ROOTING MEDIUM

Instead of rooting your leaves in water, you may want to try starting them in a rooting medium, such as sand, vermiculite, or some other mixture. You will find that your violets will be slower sprouting than in water, but they will grow a better root system and will be less affected by the change when the time comes to separate them.

Sand or vermiculite makes the most reliable starting medium. Of these two, the choice probably should favor vermiculite, but you should have good success with sand. If you use the latter, sterilize it with boiling water, as described earlier.

Many people have found redwood leaf mold to be an excellent starting medium. One of its strongest advocates asserts that she has never lost a leaf planted in this material. You may find it difficult to obtain, however, in some localities.

Setting Stems

Before setting the stems in the starting medium, dust them lightly with a rooting hormone. This will not make the leaves form roots any faster, but it does encourage them to grow a larger and heavier set of roots. But be careful not to use too much, as it can burn the stems and cause them to rot. The directions say to shake off the excess powder, but that is not enough. *Brush* if off so clean that you can barely tell that there is any on the stem, just the merest suspicion that there *has* been some.

Tests made with rooting hormones seem to prove that these hormones will often cause the leaf to grow a larger set of roots, but fewer plantlets will form than will be produced by untreated leaves.

Set the stems about 1 inch into the starting medium and place them about 2 inches apart. Mark each leaf with the variety name, as previously described, and if any refuse to stand up properly, brace them with toothpicks or broomstraws. Set them in a warm place in a good light, keep them moist but not sloppy wet.

Containers

You can choose among several types of containers for rooting your leaves.

A container made of a non-porous material, such as glass, will retain the moisture and reduce the amount of watering you may have to do.

A large goldfish bowl makes an excellent miniature greenhouse. Put about 4 inches of starting medium in the bottom and keep the top of the bowl covered for the first few days. Do not keep the cover on too tightly, however, for the leaves are apt to mildew if confined. Watch the cover, and when drops form on the underside, remove it and wipe dry. Leave it off an hour or so before replacing.

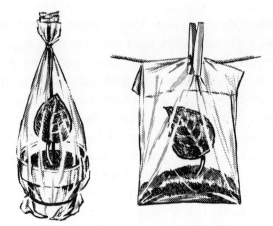

Two methods of rooting leaves, in vermiculite and plastic bags

One handy way to start leaves is to put them in transparent plastic bags. Put the leaf in two tablespoons of vermiculite in the bottom of a small plastic bag, moisten the vermiculite, and hang the bag by a clothespin or paper clip to a stout string, or thumbtack it to a shelf edge. Some growers cut a small hole in the bag for ventilation, but I have not found this necessary.

Another method is to plant a leaf in a pot of vermiculite, water it, place a small stick upright in the center, and place the pot in a bag. Fasten a string or rubber band around both the pot and the top of the bag, and stand it on a shelf.

For a smaller crop of leaves, use any handy wide-mouthed glass jar. A 1-pound peanut butter jar will hold about four or five leaves.

A satisfactory porous container that you may want to try is the pot-within-a-pot arrangement. Put a cork in the drainage hole of a 2-inch pot, and set it in the center of a 6- or 8-inch pot. Fill in the area between the two pots with your rooting medium and, having watered it thoroughly, set a row of leaves around it about an inch apart. Keep the corked pot full of water. In theory, the water in the center pot passes through the earthenware and keeps the rooting medium moist but not too wet. However, you will find that you will have to water the medium occasionally anyway.

Fertilizer and Plant Food

When the tiny plants appear above the soil, you can either encourage them with fertilizer or plant food or you can leave them alone until they grow large enough to separate. Authorities differ on this point. Some growers contend that the plants should not be fed at this stage because the nitrogen injures the roots. Others recommend feeding them every two weeks with a liquid plant food of the acid variety. One successful California grower sets his leaves in straight vermiculite and starts feeding them a week later with a complete liquid fertilizer. He keeps up the feeding on a 10-day schedule, and he produces fine plants in 2-inch pots, with an 8-inch spread of top and plenty of large blooms.

Of course, if you try this way of growing them, you must remember to make the fertilizer solution very weak for young plants.

Sometimes, a leaf planted in pure vermiculite will grow a fine crop of roots, and the leaf itself will grow much larger, but no little leaves will appear. If your leaf looks healthy but does not send up some sprouts within a reasonable time, at least within three months, take it out of the vermiculite, cut off the roots, and put the leaf either in a bottle of water until leaves appear, or else plant it in a mixture of equal parts of sand, peat, and vermiculite. This change will usually start some growth. Keep the leaves in the rooting medium until the young plants are big enough to be separated.

If you split the stem up for half an inch or so both of the split ends will usually root, and this will give you a larger number of small plants.

Leaves which are not full grown will often grow to full size after rooting, before sending up any plants.

If a leaf is cracked or broken only part way across, its split edges can be held together with a bit of adhesive tape.

One little bit of information not generally known is that leaves ship much better dry than wet. Do not put wet cotton or moss on the stems; leave them dry. They are much less likely to rot en route. If they are wilted or limp on arrival, take a sharp knife and cut off about a quarter of an inch of stem, and stand the leaves in water until they are crisp. Then let them dry for an hour or so before planting. *This does not apply to rooted leaves.*

A good way to crisp leaves is to lay them face up on a saucer or small plate, and pour in water until the stems and backs of the leaves are immersed.

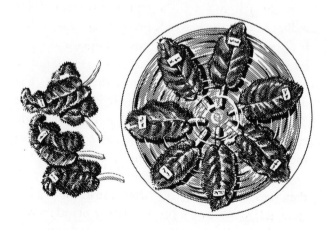

To crisp violet leaves after shipment, lay them face up in a saucer of water

CHAPTER THREE

Potting Young Plants

So your leaves have rooted nicely, and each leaf has a cluster of little plants growing from it. What should you do with it next?

When the largest of the little plants are about two inches high, they are ready for their first real potting — and here is the point where many people lose plants.

At least two weeks before you intend to pot them you should prepare your potting soil. If you do not have a pet formula of your own, read the chapter on potting soils and select one. Be sure that your soil is properly sterilized, as described in that chapter.

POTTING PARAPHERNALIA

If you have a greenhouse complete with potting bench, you will of course want to do your potting there, but otherwise the kitchen sink makes an excellent substitute. Spread several thicknesses of newspapers on the drainboard, and provide yourself with the necessary number of 2-inch pots which, of course, you have already scrubbed and sterilized, and rimmed with either wax or aluminum foil. You will also need, besides the prepared soil, a large pan with a couple of inches of warm water in it; a supply of the sand, vermiculite, or whatever it is that your leaves are already growing in; a teaspoon; a tablespoon; an old table fork; labels, pencil, a box of toothpicks; 1-inch squares of plastic screen; and a small sharp knife. A paring knife is a good size for this purpose.

Adjust the warm water faucet so that the water will drip moderately fast, but not run in a stream, and leave it that way.

SEPARATING THE PLANTS

Take up a rooted leaf with all its sprouts and lay it on the newspaper in front of you. If the parent leaf is still plump and green, and you want more plants of that kind, try to cut it loose from the plants with a few roots still on its stem, and replant. If you cannot get it out with any roots, cut it off clean with the knife, and reroot.

Separate the little plants and make a label for each one. When you separate the plants, you will probably find yourself with a few rather large ones and a number that are too small to handle easily. In that case only take off the larger ones. Leave the small ones still attached to the leaf, replant it, and let them grow until they are larger.

If some of the plants that are big enough to live alone do not have any roots of their own, you can root them in sand, vermiculite, or water, just as you would root the leaf.

Sometimes, instead of sending up plants from the end of the stem, a leaf will sprout tiny plants along the stem, or even on the edge of the leaf. Let them grow that way as long as the leaf remains alive, and when it begins to die, take them off and root them if they are big enough. A good way is to put some vermiculite or sand in a covered glass dish, dampen it well, set the tiny plants in it, and keep the cover on until they form roots.

SETTING PLANTS IN POTS

Take one of the prepared pots. Ram a square of screen down tightly in the bottom of the pot, and put 1 tablespoon of the potting soil in the pot. You can use a piece of broken pot or a pebble to cover the drainage hole if you do not have any plastic screen. On top of this put a teaspoonful of the rooting medium in which the plant has been growing. Set the baby plant on this, hold it in position in the center of the pot, and fill in around it with the rooting medium. This is so that the sudden change of soil will not burn the new roots or shock the young plants. The new and richer soil is now underneath the plant, where the roots will presently grow down to it. Take care not to cover the crown, or heart, of the plant.

One very successful grower disagrees with this point, and uses the rich potting soil throughout. But you will probably be wise to stay on the safe side, and not take a chance on burning the tender new roots.

Now hold the pot under the dripping faucet, and let the drops pat the soil down around the roots. Do not ram it down with your fingers. After all the time and trouble you have taken to grow these little roots, you do not want to break them off. Next set the pot in the pan of warm water and leave it there until thoroughly soaked, then set it in the shade.

If the plant wobbles and does not want to stand up straight, brace it with two or three toothpicks until it grows enough roots to keep it in place.

Keep the soil moist but not sloppy wet. It is better to water it from the top for the first few days, until the soil is well settled around the roots. Always use warm water, and do not stand the plant in a draft.

As the soil settles down around the roots, you may need to add a bit more to keep them covered, but be careful not to cover the crown. Leave the plant in the small pot until the roots show at the drainage hole, then you can move it to the 3-inch size. This time you can use your regular potting soil all the way through. If other conditions are favorable, the plant will bloom before it is necessary to move it to a larger pot.

There is a great deal of argument as to whether a young plant should have any fertilizer in the first potting soil or not. Some growers use Georgia peat (acid-type peat) in this first potting soil, but others think it too strong for very young plants.

Once, I conducted a limited test on twenty plants to see how different growing mediums affected the rate of growth up to the first blooming. The little plants were all the same age and size, about an inch tall, all planted in 2-inch pots. I put five in straight vermiculite, five in equal parts of vermiculite and leaf mold, five in equal parts of vermiculite and Georgia peat, and the other five in a regular potting mixture. None of them had any liquid fertilizer. I set them all on the same shelf in a south window.

The first plant to bloom was one in straight vermiculite. The second and third, a month later were in vermiculite and Georgia peat. The plants in vermiculite and leaf mold were another month later, and those in potting mixture last of all.

CHAPTER FOUR

How to Propagate by Division

A tried-and-true method for increasing the size of your violet collection and improving its quality, is, simply, to take apart some of your mature plants and to replant the pieces. This is easily done if you have a young plant with several "crowns" or an old-timer that has developed branches or suckers. In the plant world, a "crown" means a growing point, or center of a cluster, and the circle of leaves that surrounds it. Thus a "multiple-crown" plant has several crowns and a "single-crown" plant has only one, like a head of lettuce.

DIVIDING YOUNG PLANTS

If your violet came from a florist, you will probably find that it has anywhere from six to a dozen crowns of varying sizes. The commercial grower necessarily requires a lot of blossoms in a hurry and all at one time. He thus plants an entire cluster from a leaf in one pot, expecting the bloom to make a generous showing. To produce a large plant full of blooms from one crown would take quite a long time, and while the plant was slowly building up its floral display, it would be adding to the nurseryman's overhead expenses.

The violet fancier knows that single-crown plants are considered the best, and since the florist's plant will not bloom again for months anyway, it can be taken apart as soon as it stops blooming, and several separate plants made from it.

First, turn it out of its pot, and carefully separate all the crowns, big and little. Plant those with root systems in your preferred potting soil in suitable-sized pots. If some of them do not have their own root system, root them just as you would a leaf, and treat them when rooted just as you would a small plant grown from a leaf.

DIVIDING OLD PLANTS

If you have a large old multiple-crown plant that is getting to look lopsided and rather ungraceful, and has suckers growing up from the base, you can take it apart and make several better-shaped plants from it.

To make new plants from an old plant, cut the old plant apart and pot top crown, side shoots, suckers

A very good way to get a plant out of a pot without ruining it is to hold the pot firmly in your left hand, insert a pencil or similar small tool in the drainage hole and push gently but firmly. The plant is turned out of the pot without damage. This works best if you used the plastic screen square in the bottom of the pot when you planted it.

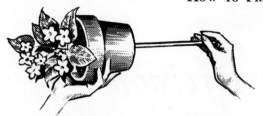

A good way to turn a plant out of a pot

First, after taking it from the pot, remove all suckers from the base with a small, sharp knife. If you can cut them off the base with some tiny roots of their own, so much the better, as they will take hold and grow more rapidly than if they have to produce an entire new set of roots. Wherever you have had to cut or break them apart, dust the cut surfaces with the slightest possible dusting of a rooting hormone. Apply it with a small brush, smaller than a lead pencil. Then pot just as you would a newly rooted leaf.

Next, remove all the side shoots at the point where they join the main stem. Root these just as you would root a leaf. They will usually root easily and soon start blooming.

This will leave the top crown and a long straggly looking main stem, often crooked, with a few leaves on it here and there. Cut it off as shown in the drawing, leaving about an inch of the stem without any leaves. You can root it in either sand or vermiculite, but if you will set it in a vase or glass of water with a very small amount of liquid fertilizer added, it will often go right on blooming. When the roots have grown out about an inch, pot the plant.

IMPROVING APPEARANCE OF AN OLD PLANT

Many people think that a violet plant is in its prime for only about a year; indeed, some magazines and books will advise you to throw it away when it is a year old and start a new one. This is a great mistake. In a recent flower show, a handsome plant which won the prize as the largest one in the show was *eight* years old.

Usually, as a violet ages it becomes ungainly owing to the fact that as it grows it sheds its lower leaves from time to time. Eventually, your pet plant may begin to resemble a small palm tree, with a bare stem and a crown on top.

To restore the plant to a more pleasing appearance, take off the lower row of leaves, and cut the plant as shown in the drawing, leaving about an inch of stem, and root it again. If the bark or skin of the stem is scarred and brown from age and shedding leaves, scrape it off very lightly with a knife in several places before setting it to root. Dust the scraped places very lightly with a rooting hormone before planting.

If the bare part of the stem is not too long, not more than a couple of inches, take it out of the pot, and cut off the bottom of the cluster of roots, scrape the bare stem very lightly and dust with a rooting hormone, then pot the entire plant, filling the soil up to about a quarter of an inch below the bottom row of leaves. The stem will send out a set of new roots from above the old roots.

When filling the soil in around the plant, a stiff paper funnel, cut off at the bottom the right size to fit between the lower leaf stems, is a great help in getting the soil into the pot without breaking off the leaves or getting soil on them.

Be careful not to water these reset plants too much at first as they are very susceptible to crown rot.

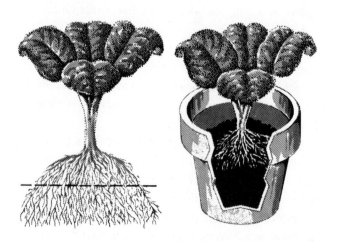

To improve appearance of top-heavy plants, cut away roots and repot deep in soil

CHAPTER FIVE

How to Grow from Seeds

To most violet enthusiasts there comes a time when they feel that they simply must grow some violets from seed. It is a fascinating hobby, and once you have grown some plants from seed, you will probably want to keep right on planting seeds, for who knows you *might* grow a prize plant!

The length of time from seed to bloom is about the same as for a plant grown from a cutting. The violets bloom in seven to ten months after the seed germinates. The length of time will depend on a number of factors, including temperature, lighting, soil conditions, size of pot, variety of seed parents, and the time of year. The best time to sow the seeds is September or October although almost any season will do.

The seedlings first appear in fourteen to twenty-one days but unless you have very good eyesight you cannot see the tiny plants without a hand glass. If they do not come up when you think they should, do not get discouraged and throw them out. They have been known to wait three or four months.

Seeds can be bought from a number of dealers —or perhaps you have a friend who can be persuaded to part with some. They are as fine as face powder and must be handled with care. A later chapter will tell you how you can grow your own.

METHODS OF SOWING SEEDS

There are almost as many ways of growing seedlings as there are saintpaulia enthusiasts who attempt it. But some methods are more certain of success than others.

One friend sows the seeds on the surface of a mixture of leaf mold and sand in almost any kind of glass container, keeps the mixture very wet and tightly covered, and sets her containers on the kitchen sink until the seeds sprout. Sometimes she stands the container on the back of her stove, and the seedlings come up as thick as cat fur. When I tried that particular method, all I grew was a luxuriant crop of gray velvet mold.

The late Harvey Cox grew seedlings very successfully in a mixture of equal parts of leaf mold and vermiculite in pint fruit jars. He used the square-type glass jar, laid on its side. He put an inch-deep layer of his mixture in the jar, firmed it down, moistened it, and then sowed the seeds on top. He then screwed on the lid and left the

Seedlings grow well in pint mason jars

plants alone until they grew large enough to touch the glass above them. He then transplanted the seedlings into foot-square flats, filled with leaf mold and sand. The seedlings were set in deep about an inch apart and the flat was covered with glass for a week or so to allow the seedlings

21

to recover from the move. When his little plants outgrew the flat, he transferred them to 2-inch pots, where they stayed until they bloomed.

Mrs. Constance Hansen also likes to use pint jars. She puts in first about a teaspoonful of charcoal, then, with the jar lying on its side, she fills it about one third with her regular potting soil, sprinkles a thin layer of vermiculite on top, moistens it thoroughly, and sows the seeds. She keeps the lid on until the plants are big enough for their first transplanting.

My favorite container for growing seedlings is a clear plastic refrigerator container about four inches square with a lid. Some brands of cottage cheese are sold in these containers, but they are also obtainable in most dime stores. They are light, easy to handle, fit neatly on the window sill, and do not break. They cannot be boiled, but can be washed with soap and water.

Seedlings also thrive in plastic boxes

After trying out all the different mediums for seedlings that are recommended by various growers, I find I am most successful when I plant the seeds in, or rather on, a finely ground form of vermiculite. It is sterile, and needs no extra care. But be sure to water it, *before* sowing the seeds, with water which has been boiled and allowed to cool.

I put an inch-deep layer in the plastic container, shake it down evenly, and sow the seeds on the surface but do not cover them. Then I put the lid on the container, set it in a warm place in a good light, but not in the sun.

If the soil was properly moistened before the seeds were sown, it probably will not need any more water until the seedlings are quite a good size. If moisture forms in drops on the underside of the lid, take off the lid, wipe it dry, and replace it. If the soil mixture dries out, it may be watered by trickling water from a teaspoon down the side of the plastic container.

Puffed rock is another good medium. Its snow-whiteness shows up the tiny green seedlings, making them easy to see. The algae that grow on the surface of this medium after a short time are said to have no harmful effect on the seedlings.

Many people like to start fine seeds on sphagnum moss. In some places it is possible to buy ground sphagnum. If not, take the dry sphagnum and put it through the kitchen food chopper, using the cutter you would use for grinding rather fine bread crumbs. Then put it in a container and pour boiling water over it, and let stand until cool. Be sure it is thoroughly soaked. Squeeze most of the water out, leaving it quite moist but not sloppy wet, put it in your seed box, firm it down a bit but do not pack it tight, and sow the seeds on the surface. Keep box closely covered, as the moss dries out very quickly if uncovered.

Some of my correspondents have great success growing violet seedlings on bricks. To do this, sterilize an ordinary porous brick by boiling, and when it has cooled, spread half an inch of vermiculite or your favorite seed-growing soil on the top side. Sow the seeds on the surface. Put the brick in a pan or other suitable container, and pour water in the container to the depth of about an inch. Keep the water level constant. Transplant the baby plants as soon as they are large enough to handle.

Another way is to start them on a sponge. Sterilize the sponge with boiling water. Lay it on a bed of charcoal in a pan or other container, and keep it constantly moist. Sow seed directly on the sponge. When just barely up, gently remove the seedlings to a container filled with a screened mixture of 1

Orchard Nursery

BLUE LADY

Lois B. Hammond

SHOW GIRL

Lois B. Hammond

ROYAL RIPPLES

Orchard Nursery

BUTTON'S 'N BOWS

23

part leaf mold, 1 part peat moss, 1/10 part vermiculite. It is not necessary to plant the seedlings, just lay them on top of the mixture, and keep it quite moist but not wet.

TRANSPLANTING THE SEEDLINGS

When they grow the fourth pair of leaves, the seedlings are ready for the first transplanting. If you can get them, 1-inch pots are nice for the first potting of young seedlings. Sterilize the pots in advance and soak them thoroughly just before using, because if they are bone-dry they will absorb the water from the potting soil and dry out the plant.

Once a week they should be watered with a very weak solution of a reliable liquid fertilizer, about one-fourth as strong as for larger plants. Some people disagree with this recommendation on the ground that the plants should not have any fertilizer until they bloom the first time. However, I have not had any trouble with fertilizing before blooms appear.

If the seedlings are very tiny, you can put from three to five in each 2-inch pot, keeping them slightly separate. Later, when they begin to crowd each other, repot them singly in 2-inch pots. Seedlings always grow much faster after they have been removed from the seed pan and replanted, either in pots or other containers.

Harden the young plants before the first potting by taking the cover off for a longer period each day until they can go uncovered for the whole day without wilting.

For the first potting use equal parts of your usual potting soil and either sponge rock or vermiculite. A regular potting mix is too strong for such baby plants, and may burn the roots.

After they are potted, stand the pots in shallow pans as close together as possible and pack vermiculite or sponge rock around them up to the rims. Some people use sphagnum moss or green moss, but it is more likely to harbor insects and molds than either vermiculite or sponge rock. Always keep this packing moist, as the small pots dry out very quickly. Keep the seedlings in these pots until the roots show at the drainage hole.

You can plant them singly or in groups of three or four in any shallow wooden box or in glass or plastic dishes, spacing about one inch apart each way. Cover with glass for the first few days, removing the cover for a longer time each day until you can leave it off entirely.

In any case, when the plants are large enough for 2-inch pots, pot them up just as you pot rooted leaf cuttings. Leave them in the 2-inch pots until they bloom the first time.

TESTING A NEW VARIETY

When they bloom, give away those that do not show signs of being really different. There are always plenty of people who do not care anything about the variety name of a violet: all they want is a nice-looking plant with some flowers on it.

If any of your plants are really different keep them for further testing. Allow them to bloom at least three times to make sure that they are going to stay different, because sometimes the second or even the third set of blooms may vary from the first.

The second important test is to root leaves from the plant and see whether they produce a plant with characteristics like the parent plant. Sometimes they will not propagate true, even though the parent plant continues to be unique. To make certain that you have produced a new variety, you should propagate to the third generation.

If the differences pass these tests, you may possibly have created a new variety, and you should apply to the African Violet Society for a registration application, as described in Chapter 11.

CHAPTER SIX

Potting Soils and Containers

Surprisingly enough, African violets can be grown in a wide range of soils. The main requirement is that the soil be somewhat granular in texture to allow excess water to drain away easily and yet not so open that it will lose all moisture between waterings.

In its native home in Africa, the saintpaulia grows in a soil mainly composed of leaf mold and decomposed rock. There are few localities in this country that can duplicate the violet's native soil in texture and composition; but in many areas, the garden soil is adequate for producing fine violet plants.

In many other areas, however, particularly the Southwest, the composition of the soil is so different from that favored by the violet, that it cannot be used, and it is necessary to mix your own to a formula.

Eastern correspondents are inclined to be a bit scornful of formulas for mixing soil. They write that they have only to go out into the back yard, the barnyard, or wood lot and scrape up some soil from under a tree or a hedge, and it produces beautiful thriving violets without any fuss or muss. But in many parts of the Southwest, the soil is adobe, a heavy clay that lacks humus. In other localities, the soil is light and sandy and lacks nearly everything. In one place where I lived, the soil would not even support healthy weeds. Throughout a good part of the West the soil is strongly alkaline; in the Northwest it tends toward acidity.

If your African violet is doing all right in its present soil, leave it alone. But if it is not thriving,

the trouble may be in the soil composition. If you are suspicious of your soil, there are several steps you can take to find out if it is unsuitable.

SOIL ALKALINITY

First step is to check on the alkalinity of your potting soil.

A neutral or slightly acid soil is thought to be best for African violets. If the soil is too alkaline, it produces a stunted, unhealthy plant with a poor root system. If it is too acid, it will cause the buds to drop before opening. Most growers think that slightly acid soil brings out better color in the pink and blue blossoms than neutral soil does.

If you do not know whether your potting soil is acid or alkaline, you can find out by sending a sample to a commercial testing laboratory that specializes in handling soil tests. In some states, the county farm bureau may analyze a sample for you. Gather representative samples from several parts of your garden, blend them thoroughly, and send off a small sample of the blend. One commercial testing laboratory requires only 4-6 ounces of soil.

Although not so accurate as a professional analysis, there is a simple test that you can make yourself that is quite helpful. Buy a tube of litmus papers from your drugstore. Water a potful of soil with distilled or rain water until the water runs out the bottom of the pot into the saucer. Dip a slip of litmus paper into the water in the saucer. If the paper turns pink, the soil is acid. If it turns blue, the soil is alkaline. This will tell you roughly on which side of the division line your soil belongs.

For a more accurate home test, you can use one of the soil-testing kits sold in garden stores.

If your soil analysis shows too much acid, you can correct this by adding a little ground limestone to the soil mixture, or by putting some limestone chips in the bottom of the pot. Or you can put limestone chips in the bottom of a container and pour boiling water over them. When the water cools sufficiently, use it on the plants.

If your soil analysis shows too much alkali, use more leaf mold, being sure to get a good grade of either oak or redwood leaf mold. Or else buy one of the commercial mixtures sold especially for African violets.

In some localities, the soil is deficient in iron. In any part of the country where an iron deficiency is known to exist, garden stores usually sell some preparation to counteract it.

For alkaline mixtures, or if you have to use hard water for your plants, the University of California recommends the use of ferrous sulphate about once every six weeks. This is a powder, obtainable from a drug store. Unless you have a great many plants, an ounce will last a long time. Use 1/4 teaspoon to 1 gallon of water, and water the plants freely with it.

POTTING MIXTURES

Some growers produce beautiful African violets in straight garden loam, some succeed with nothing but vermiculite or crushed pumice, but most fanciers depend on a potting mixture.

There are almost as many formulas for potting mixtures as there are violet growers. Most of them, however, are built around four basic ingredients:

1. Sterilized garden soil (sometimes omitted).
2. A soil lightener, such as sand, vermiculite, or crushed pumice.
3. An acid humus, such as leaf mold or acid-type peat.
4. A slow-acting fertilizer, such as manure, bonemeal, or superphosphate.

The proportions in which these are combined will vary according to local soil conditions, type of blooms desired, or, sometimes, personal whim of the grower.

If your pet formula is no longer producing satisfactory results, you may want to experiment with formulas that other growers have used successfully. Here are several for you to try:

A standard soil mixture is the following:
1 part sheep or cow manure
2 parts builder's sand
3 parts leaf mold
4 parts good garden soil

To each quart, add 1 tablespoon of bonemeal and 1/2 tablespoon of superphosphate. When you are ready to use it, add 1 tablespoon of chick charcoal to each 4-inch potful. You can buy this type charcoal in any poultry supply store and in nurseries or garden stores.

Another popular variation of this formula is:
2 parts sheep or cow manure
2 parts builder's sand
4 parts leaf mold
4 parts good garden soil

Add 2 tablespoons of bonemeal and 4 tablespoons of charcoal to each quart of the mixture after sterilizing.

Mrs. Constance Hansen recommends:
5 parts live-oak leaf mold
1 part crushed pumice
A small amount of bonemeal

She supplements this with a feeding of liquid fertilizer every two weeks.

Mrs. Clarissa Harris, well known as the originator of the popular variety Marine, recommends this mixture:
4 parts leaf mold
2 parts manure
2 parts sand
2 parts peat moss or vermiculite
1 part charcoal
1/2 part bonemeal

Here is an unorthodox formula favored by the late Harvey Cox:

    9 parts leaf mold
    5 parts loam
    2 parts sharp sand
Sterilize and add:
    3 parts coarse vermiculite
    ½ part bonemeal
    ½ part charcoal

An acid planting mix which is said to counteract the hard water which some of us have to use on our violets is made as follows:

    8 parts clean coarse sand
    1 part acid peat
To each bushel of this mixture add:
    6 tablespoons hoof and horn meal (buy it from an orchid grower)
    7 tablespoons superphosphate
    1 tablespoon sulfate of potash
    7½ tablespoons dolomite lime

A Canadian correspondent writes that a favorite formula in his part of the country is:

    1 part sharp sand
    1 part leaf mold
    1 part peat moss
    1 part good garden soil

In localities where the temperature and humidity are both very high, the loss of plants from root or crown rot is apt to be correspondingly high, especially in summer. In such places it is a good idea to use a very light soil mix, mostly sand and leaf mold. Fill pots at least a third of the way up with chick charcoal, and then with the soil mix. Water them *very* sparingly in hot weather. There is nothing that will kill violets faster than constantly soggy soil.

STERILIZING POTTING SOIL

As a protection against the pests and diseases that thrive in most garden soils, it is prudent to sterilize all soil used in potting. By the time your plants are ready for their final potting, they should be sturdy enough to ward off most ailments that may be transmitted through the soil, but sterilization will insure that they will not have to cope with fungus, nema-todes, and other soil-borne pests. You can save yourself a great deal of trouble by sterilizing your soil before using it.

Usually, sterilizing only the soil is sufficient protection, although some growers sterilize the entire potting mixture. This will protect the plant from pests and diseases carried by the manure, peat, or leaf mold; but it may also reduce the value of some of these elements. For example, heat will release the nitrogen from the manure.

Some people object to sterilizing potting soil because they say the beneficial fungi and bacteria are destroyed as well as the harmful organisms. This might be true if you were able to *completely* sterilize your soil, but the processes available to you are not likely to do more than partially sterilize it. Most Californians, at least, would rather sterilize soil than do battle with the numerous pests and diseases that flourish in some of our soils.

Potting soil should be sterilized well in advance of potting day, since it takes the soil several days to recover its texture. Preferably, it should be sterilized two weeks before it is blended into the potting mixture.

There are several ways to treat the soil. If you wish to sterilize it by chemical means, you can choose from a variety of effective fumigants and soil sterilants. As new products are constantly being developed in this field, you would do well to ask your nurseryman to recommend a reliable product.

You will probably find that the easiest methods for you to use are to steam the soil in your pressure canner or to bake it in the oven.

To sterilize the soil in a pressure canner, first place the rack in the canner as if you were going to can fruit, and pour in the proper amount of water. Then put the soil in a container that will fit loosely inside the canner and leave space all around for the steam. Set the container full of soil inside the canner on top of the wire rack. Do not cover the container. Put the lid on the canner and give it 5 pounds pressure for 15 minutes. Remove the container and pour boiling water over the soil to moisten it thoroughly and stir it well.

Lois B. Hammond

EXCELSIS

Shaffer's Tropical Gardens

VELVET GIRL

Lois B. Hammond

JUNO

Orchard Nursery

ENCHANTRESS

To bake the potting soil in your oven, place it in a pan and set it in the oven for 2½ hours at 250 degrees. If your oven does not have heat control, then bake the soil with the flame turned low, as you would set it to bake a delicate custard. Put enough water in the pan to come almost to the top of the soil, and cover the pan while baking. Afterward, let it stand uncovered in a place where it will not be in contact with infected plants or unsterilized dirt. Stir it well every day or so and keep it moist. Do not use for a week after baking.

Small quantities may be sterilized in a double boiler, as described in the chapter on planting seeds.

To replace the nitrogen that has been released by the baking process, it is usually a good idea occasionally to apply a fertilizer with a rather high nitrogen percentage. But do not use it all the time, or you will grow more leaves than either flowers or roots.

If your soil has a tendency to pack down hard or bake solid, buy one of the soil conditioners obtainable under various trade names, and mix it with the soil at the rate recommended on the package. Mix thoroughly, moisten the soil well, and let it stand 24 hours. The soil will then be ready for use. Don't forget, however, that soil conditioners are *not* fertilizers.

POTS AND CONTAINERS

Violets can be grown in almost any kind of container, from a jelly glass to a tin can. But they do their best when treated to a good, clean clay pot of the proper size.

Types of Pots

There are very colorful plastic pots on the market, and though some people use them quite successfully, you will probably find that your plants will grow better in porous pots. The plastic pots do not seem to admit sufficient air to the roots, and unless the soil mixture is very coarse and porous, the plant is likely to succumb to crown rot.

The same criticism applies to glazed pottery pots. Although they are certainly much better looking than the plain unglazed variety, they demand very, very careful control of watering, otherwise crown rot is likely to set in. This is not to say that they cannot or should not be used, but it is safer for the beginner to practice with the porous pots until sure how much water to use before risking any pet plants in non-porous vessels.

Many people like to grow the smaller or more delicate varieties in bubble bowls, but they are very careful about selecting a soil mixture and even more careful about watering the rooted plants. There are several mixtures on the market that are specially prepared for growing plants in containers without drainage. These mixtures are quite suitable for general potting of violets in any kind of pot, but being very light and porous in texture, they are particularly adapted to bubble bowls and similar containers. If you set your plant in a bubble bowl, you will find it a good idea to put an inch layer of vermiculite on top of the potting mixture. The crust of vermiculite will make it easy for you to tell if the plant needs watering. If you tip the bowl or shake it gently and the vermiculite rolls a bit on top, that is the signal to add water. If it does not roll, the mixture is damp enough.

Strawberry Jar

A planting in a strawberry jar always attracts attention, and if properly planted and trained it can be

Strawberry jar is attractive container for violets

very beautiful. It is advisable to choose plants of the same habit and rate of growth. Select those that have rather short stems and a compact head and which grow to about the same size at maturity. For if one of the plants gets much larger than the rest, with larger leaves and longer stems, the symmetry of the planting is destroyed and the whole piece looks lopsided.

Personally, I prefer to drill a hole in the bottom of the jar for drainage; but it is possible to use it without a drainage hole, if you are very careful about watering. In either case, put a 2-inch layer of drainage material, such as chick charcoal, in the bottom, and then fill with the soil to the first row of pockets. Plant the first row of plants in the pockets with the roots pointed toward the middle, and fill in soil to the second row of openings. Water down and let stand two or three days to settle.

Next, insert an open core in the center to admit water and air. Use an aluminum tube, a stack of 2-inch pots tall enough to reach almost to the top of the jar, or a cardboard tube such as comes in the middle of a roll of paper towels. Finally, put in the next row of plants, and fill as before, until you have filled to within a couple of inches of the top of the jar.

If you used an aluminum tube, fill it up with coarse gravel. The cardboard tube should not be left in place permanently. After you have filled soil around it, press the mixture firmly around the tube. Then give the tube a twist or two to firm the wall of soil around it, and remove it. Fill the hole left with gravel or chick charcoal.

If the jar is a large one, with ample room at the top, you can plant from one to three plants in the top opening, but if the jar is small, it should not be filled up quite so far. Fit a potted plant into the opening at the top.

Soil mixture used in this kind of planting should be very light and porous, or you may have trouble from sour soil and too little air.

This planting should be turned at least twice a week, and it is really better to give it a quarter turn every day. Any leaves which grow out crooked or crowd the plant next to them should either be trained to shape or picked off.

Size of Pots

Although doubtless there are people who will disagree with me, experience and observation have convinced me that the proper-sized pots for African violets are the smallest sized ones that will hold the plants. This opinion has been confirmed by several of the most successful growers in California. These are the reasons:

African violets will bloom better when slightly pot-bound.

The seedlings and rooted cuttings will bloom when much younger if kept in small pots.

The pots take up less room on the plant shelf, which is quite a recommendation if you are short of display space.

The plants are not so likely to develop crown rot, because there is less soil to become soggy and sour if over-watered.

Any plant that is healthy and doing well need not be repotted until its roots appear at the drainage hole. It should then be shifted to the next larger size. Start off your small plants in 2-inch pots and leave them alone until they bloom or until the roots show at the bottom. Then move them to 3-inch pots and leave them there quite a long time. The final potting should be in 4-inch pots. By the time they have outgrown this size, the plants will probably have developed a long stem and should be cut down as described in the chapter on dividing plants. There are a few varieties, however, that do not grow long stems and tend to grow outward rather than upward. For such special cases, you will probably want to use a pot larger than the 4-inch.

CHAPTER SEVEN

Methods of Watering

Whenever I speak before a club about watering African violets, I always find that there is at least one person in the audience who grows violets in pots that are constantly standing in water anywhere from one to three inches deep, has done so for years, has never lost a plant, and has the finest violets in the neighborhood, and wants to know how I account for that.

I don't account for it. Such procedure is completely contrary to all the accepted rules for culture of the saintpaulia, which is not an aquatic plant, and which will usually curl up and die if watered too freely.

There is another violet fancier who waters the plants once a week on a certain day, regardless of weather conditions or the size of the plant. She never mentions losing one.

If you would like to try either of these methods, you might practice them first on some plants that you consider expendable, so that if they die you will not be discouraged.

The basic rules about watering—that these growers claim to violate so successfully—are simple and easy to follow. These are: Soak the plants thoroughly with *warm* water, let the surplus drain off, and if any is left in the pot saucers after an hour or so, pour it out, do not let the plants stand in it. Then do not water again until the surface is dry to the touch. And I mean DRY.

When I say "dry surface," I mean exactly dry *surface*. Never let your plant get bone dry clear to the bottom of the pot. If you allow the soil in the pot to dry out until it shrinks away from the side,

there is danger that when you water it from the top, the water will run through so fast that the soil in the middle around the roots will remain dry and the plant will thirst for water, even though the surface looks wet and water is running out at the bottom.

Only the first half inch below the surface in 2-inch pots, and about an inch below the surface in large pots should be allowed to get really dry.

The frequency with which they should be watered depends on the size of the pot, the porousness of the soil, the variety of the plant, the time of the year, and the conditions under which they are grown. Some individual plants will take more water than others. And if the humidity in your house is high, the plants will not take up as much water as they will when the humidity is low.

TOP VS. BOTTOM WATERING

The time-honored method of watering violets, which is usually recommended to the beginner, is always to water from the bottom by standing the pot in a pan of water until dampness shows on the surface of the soil in the pot. This is a very good way, particularly if you have only one or two plants. But it is a bothersome method to follow if you have a large number of violets. With a large collection, you would have to spend most of your time dunking potted violets in pans of water.

Actually, if you are careful, you can water violets from the top, like any other house plant. Use a watering can with a long thin spout that can nose in under the leaves. With it, you can pour water gently on the soil around the plant, taking care not to pour any into the center of the crown.

In localities where the water is hard, it is preferable to water from the top.

If you have hard water it is better to water from the top. It is also advisable to add an agent, such as ferrous sulphate, to counteract the hard water.

WICK WATERING

Wick watering is a trouble-free and successful way of keeping your violets adequately irrigated. If you would like to try it, obtain a piece of fiberglass wicking, about the size of twine, cut off a 4-inch piece, and draw one end of it through the drainage hole of a pot. You do not need any special pots for this system, although you can buy them if you wish. Spread out the end inside the pot until it lies flat all around the hole. This will keep it from slipping out. Then put in your soil and plant as usual. Water

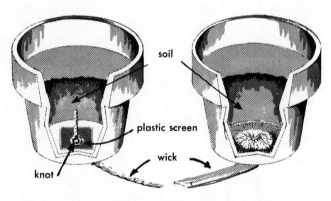

To hold wick inside pot, place plastic screen over hole, knot wick. Or, spread end of wick inside pot

the plant from the top until water comes through and drips from the end of the wick. Then rest the pot in a saucer or container that is made so it will hold a few inches of water and support the potted plant so its bottom rests an inch or so above the surface of the water. The bottom of the pot must not touch the water in the lower container. There must always be an air space between the bottom of the pot and the water.

About every two weeks, empty out the water from the bottom vessel and let the plant dry until the surface soil is quite dry. Thoroughly clean the bottom container and refill with water or solution. Then water the plant until it drips from the wick and put it back in place.

Although there is some danger of crown rot in this method, many people prefer it. One of the secrets of successful wick watering is not to use too fat wicks, which keep the plant too wet. For a plant of 4-inch pot size or smaller, a wick about the size of twine is sufficient. For very large plants, a fatter wick may be safely used.

CONSTANT WATER-LEVEL METHOD

The constant water-level method is used by some growers. Here is the way to work it:

Obtain a water-tight pan or trough not less than 6 inches deep. The length and width will depend on the size of the space where you plan to put it. If the container is of metal, paint the inside with asphalt paint.

Place a 2-inch layer of small pebbles on the bottom, and in one corner set a small empty porous pot. Place the pot *on top* of the layer of pebbles.

Next, place a 1-inch layer of coarse sand on top of the pebbles, flood it with water, and level it. After it is level, draw off excess water with a small rubber syringe or a grease skimmer. Draw the water out through the empty pot.

Place the potted plants (in porous pots) on top of the sand and press them very slightly into it to create contact. Build up sand around the outside of the pots, flood with water, and drain off the excess through the empty pot in the corner. This creates a seal around the pots. Vary the depth of the sand according to the dryness of your room; that is, in a dry room you would bank the sand close to the brim of the pots, in a moist climate or season, you would use less sand.

Water the pots the first time from the top to establish capillarity. Thereafter, water through the small empty pot, keeping the water level at the *bottom* of the pot, or, in other words, until the water *starts* to come through the drainage hole. Do not let it come any higher. Check and water daily.

When the soil on top of a pot becomes dry, water it from the top to establish capillarity. If a pot is taken out and replaced, both the capillarity and the seal around the pot must be re-established by pouring water on the pot and the surrounding sand.

WATER CONDITION

As explained in a previous chapter, water that is chemically pure is ideal for African violets. However, obtaining this in sufficient quantity to satisfy a thirsty collection of mature plants is sometimes a problem. Rain water and melted snow are perfect, but these sources cannot be depended upon for a steady supply in most regions.

Most of us have to rely upon the water that runs out of the kitchen faucet, and in some localities it is not too friendly to African violets. If your tap water is hard, as it is in many areas in the Southwest, you can correct it by adding an acidifier such as cider vinegar, ferrous sulphate, or one of the other commercial preparations available at your nursery or garden store. If you use vinegar, add 1 tablespoon to a gallon of water; if you use a commercial acidifier, follow directions on the container. Water your plants with the acid solution about once every six weeks. If you have a large number of plants, you will probably find the acidifier cheaper than the vinegar.

If you do not know whether your water is hard, test it with litmus papers. It may be considered hard if it produces an alkaline reaction in the test papers. Your city water department can quickly tell you exactly how hard your tap water is.

In cities where water is chlorinated, draw it the day before and let it stand 24 hours before using.

If you have a water softener attached to the plumbing, never use the softened water on your violets. It will kill them. It is better to use hard water and correct with an acidifier.

VACATION WATERING

If you are going to be away for a week or two, you can leave your plants at home with peace of mind if you make some simple provisions for them to "water" themselves while you are away.

Here are three tested methods to slow down the drying out:

1. Soak some bricks in a tub of water overnight, then drain out water until surface is an inch below the top surface of the bricks. Water your potted plants, and set them on top of the bricks, close together. This scheme is reported to keep the soil moist for two weeks.

2. Saturate several thicknesses of newspapers, water your potted plants, and set them on top of the papers, placing them close together. This too should keep your plants fresh for a couple of weeks.

3. Sink your pots to the rim in a packing of wet sand or sawdust. Saturate the packing and water the potted plants. This method should keep your plants fresh for three to six weeks.

Soaked bricks or newspapers will hold water and keep plants moist during vacation

It is important that the room in which the plants are left be well ventilated. Otherwise, crown rot or mildew will result from all this moisture.

Plastic

Another method for insuring that your plants will not dry out while you are away is to cover them with a plastic tent. Here's how:

Before going on a vacation, go over every plant and pick off every limp or fading leaf, all dead flowers and stems, and every bud that is large enough to open before you return. If any dead or limp leaves, stems, or flowers are left on the plants, they will mold or rot. Make sure that no leaves or stems are on the surface of the soil in the pot.

Water the plants moderately.

The next day, insert several tall slender sticks around the edges of the pot. These are to keep the plastic from settling down on the plant. For sticks I use the round wooden applicators without cotton, which you can get at any drug store.

Take a large sheet of clear plastic refrigerator wrap, and cover the plant and pot, fairly closely, but not absolutely air tight. If the plants are small, you can put them in a pan or tray and cover from six to twelve with one cover.

I have kept plants this way for three weeks in good condition, in moderate weather, but I cannot say what a heat wave would do to them. Try a few expendables first and see what success you have.

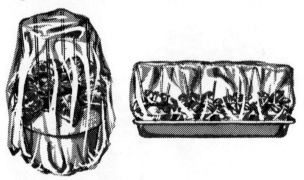

Another way to keep plants moist is to cover pot or tray of violets with plastic wrap

WASHING VIOLETS

You may have been told that you must never get any water on the leaves of an African violet. Don't believe it. Washing them when they get dusty is just as good for them as it is for you. In their native habitat the rainfall is above 70 inches a year.

This is what you should remember about washing

them: always use warm water and do not stand them in a draft or let the sun shine on the leaves while wet. If you chance to sprinkle them with cold water, or water that is even slightly cooler than room temperature, their leaves will develop ring spots.

To protect the pot and roots while washing the leaves, take a piece of flexible plastic material about a foot square for a 4-inch pot, or smaller for a smaller pot, and cut a slit from one outer edge to the center. Slip it around the stem of the plant and wrap it around the pot to keep soil from washing out.

When washing leaves, protect roots with flexible plastic material wrapped about stem and pot

The plants should be rinsed until the water washes all the dust off the leaves. The simplest way to wash a few plants is to hold them one at a time under the warm water faucet, tipping them sideways so the water strikes the center of the plant and runs outward, and turning them so all the leaves will be washed. Use a fairly gentle stream and take care that the water does not get too warm. Afterwards, place them in a warm dry spot, away from sun and drafts, until the leaves dry out.

A spray attachment, such as the kind you can attach to the mixing faucet on your kitchen sink, is a handy device for washing violets.

Once every two weeks, spray with an insecticide. See the chapter on pests and diseases for recommended sprays.

CHAPTER EIGHT

Fertilizers and Nutrient Solutions

Your pet violet will respond to a careful program of fertilizing. In time, most potted plants suffer to some degree from the artificiality of their soil condition. As the roots fill the container, they exhaust the soil and it cannot enrich itself through natural processes as it does in the garden. To keep the plant from eventually exhausting its restricted supply of earth, a little nutrient should be added from time to time. The plant will respond with lovelier blooms or heavier foliage.

In fact, it is possible to support the plant on nothing but nutrient, and dispense with the soil altogether or just use it as a means of holding the nutrient. More about that a little later. But first, let us discuss fertilizers.

FERTILIZERS

There are a number of excellent soluble fertilizers on the market that you can use. Almost any fertilizer recommended for begonias will do very well for violets. Some are better for use with hard water than others. Some will grow beautiful foliage, but not many blossoms. If you want flowers, look for a formula on the container that gives a low percentage of nitrogen and a higher percentage of phosphoric acid. If you want to develop foliage, use a formula that is strong in nitrates.

But do watch your step. You can overdo fertilizers and damage the plants. Be careful not to overdose. A single tablespoonful of solution, prepared according to the directions on the container, is usually enough for a plant in a 2-inch pot, and two tablespoonfuls for a 3-inch pot. A 4-inch pot can take a quarter of a cup.

Never give your plants any kind of fertilizer when the soil is dry. Always water at least two hours beforehand with plain water. Apply fertilizer from the top, being careful not to get it on the leaves or in the crown. Do not stand the plant in a pan of fertilizer solution, for this is likely to kill it.

Sheep, cow, or steer manure is an excellent plant food, but many people find it difficult to know when they are using it in the proper strength. Should you want to use it, place a handful of processed manure in a quart container and pour boiling water over it. Let cool and strain. Dilute with water until it reaches the color of weak tea before using.

If you have potted your plant into a fairly rich soil it probably will not need any fertilizer for six months or so. After that you can feed it about once every two weeks or once a month, depending on whether your plant is a large one in a small pot, or a small one without much top. The bigger the plant, the more fertilizer it will require.

Some authorities advise against fertilizing young plants until they have finished their first blooming. But many successful growers begin feeding liquid fertilizer from the time they get their first true leaves.

You will probably find it helpful to work out your fertilizing program on a systematic basis. Here is a system developed by experienced growers that you might like to try:

1st week ammonium sulfate (1 tsp. to 1 qt. water)

2nd week superphosphate (1 tsp. to 1 qt. water)

3rd week complete fertilizer ($\frac{1}{4}$ tsp. to 1 qt. water)

This treatment should be given four times a year.

An easier program is simply to feed a liquid fertilizer to the plants every two to four weeks (¼ tsp. to 1 qt. water).

You do not need to fertilize regularly throughout the entire year. In fact, if you were to do so, you would probably spoil your plants. Give them a rest. Don't add fertilizer when the plant is dormant or when room temperature is below 70 degrees.

You will no doubt notice, in garden stores and also in dime stores, preparations on sale for use on African violets which are advertised as "bloom boosters." Some of them are very good — but do not make the mistake of overdoing their application. They are for temporary use on plants which stubbornly refuse to bloom, and should not be used over long periods of time. There is a very simple booster that you can mix yourself which is effective and harmless if properly applied. To make it, put 1 teaspoonful of fish emulsion and 1 teaspoonful of acid plant food in 1 gallon of water, and mix thoroughly. Use this every two weeks until you have used it three times. It almost always works; but do not keep on using it indefinitely.

NUTRIENT SOLUTIONS

It is possible to dispense with soil mixtures altogether and grow your African violet in a solution that contains all the nutrients found in soil.

A mature violet will grow for some time and even blossom in water alone; it will do better in water enriched occasionally with fertilizers, but it will not do as well as it would if potted in soil unless it is kept in contact with a nutrient solution. These solutions are made up from special preparations sold for this purpose under various trade names.

The nutrient preparation differs from a fertilizer in that it contains all the elements found in a balanced fertilizer (nitrogen, potash, phosphorous) plus the minor elements needed to sustain life (magnesium, iron, etc.). Some complete fertilizers also contain these minor elements and may be used in a nutrient solution. However, most fertilizers do not contain all the elements needed for this purpose.

Nutrient preparations are usually mixed with water. The kind of water available may make some difference in the results. The ideal water of course is free from any of the chemicals that may form an unfortunate combination with the elements in the preparation; so it is best to use distilled water, rain water, or melted snow if obtainable. However, some people succeed with tap water.

There are two ways of bringing this solution into contact with the roots: in one the plant is grown in a container that is filled with liquids only, in another it is grown in a neutral sand or gravel that serves as a holding medium for the solution.

For growing in liquids alone, use any water-tight container that is not made of metal and that is preferably light-proof. When you have rooted an old, cut-off crown in a glass of water you can go right on growing it in the same glass, but you should take it out of the glass every two or three weeks, rinse roots with plain warm water, scrub and sterilize the glass, and refill it with nutrient solution and replace the plant. Even so, in the course of time, algae will form on the roots. It is therefore better to use a container that the light cannot penetrate.

Sand or gravel culture is another form of this same method. In this case the plant is planted in sterilized sand or gravel which has been moistened — not flooded — with solution.

At least once a month the sand should be removed and washed in clear water. You can do this by pouring in enough water so that the plant floats, then lift it out and lay it to one side. Pour the sand and water through a fine sieve, and run enough water through it to wash the sand clean. Scrub the bowl or container. Then replace part of the sand, set the plant on it, and put in the rest of the sand. Add enough solution so that the plant roots will adjust themselves when the container is jiggled gently.

FOLIAR FEEDING

Foliar feeding (feeding through the leaves) is practiced on a variety of plants, principally trees and shrubs. The objection to its use on violets is that if they are grown in a good soil mixture and

Orchard Nursery

MOUNT HOOD

Orchard Nursery

JIVARO

Lois B. Hammond

White seedling: PURITY X PINK DELIGHT

Lois B. Hammond

Blue seedling: NEPTUNE X PINK GIRL

Lois B. Hammond

PINK DELIGHT

Shaffer's Tropical Gardens

CALIFORNIA CASCADE

kept properly fed, they do not need foliar feeding. Nevertheless, there are times when this type of feeding is useful.

A newly set plant that has not yet become established can be given a decided boost by a few feedings, and with less danger of damaging the roots than by feeding it in the usual manner. Plants that you wish to keep in a small container can remain in it longer if they occasionally get a little extra food through their leaves. Or a plant which is at a standstill, although perfectly healthy, can often be persuaded to wake up by foliar feeding.

Several of the plant foods used by violet fanciers are adaptable to foliar application, and there are others that are compounded specifically for the purpose. It is advisable to make the solution much weaker than for root feeding, and if possible use distilled water in mixing it. Spray the plants once or twice a week with it, as much as possible on the *under* side of the leaves. Of course, the treated plants must be kept out of the sun and drafts until

dry, and the temperature of the room should be 70 degrees or over, or the treatment will not be effective.

ALWAYS REMEMBER:

1. Cut the fertilizer to one-half the strength of directions given for other house plants under glass.

2. Except when using bloom boosters, feed plants only when they are budding or in bloom.

3. Never fertilize a bone-dry plant.

4. Feed plants the same day each week or month.

5. Always use lukewarm water when fertilizing or watering.

6. Choose a fertilizer that does not burn the foliage. Any spray fertilizer is apt to burn leaves if room temperature is above 80 degrees.

7. Too much fertilizer causes distorted centers and/or leaves. To correct, stand the pot on a rack and pour over the plant at least a pint of warm water, letting it run through and drain thoroughly. Use no more fertilizer until the plant has started to grow.

CHAPTER NINE

Light, Temperature and Humidity

The growth and prospering of your African violet depends on its receiving the proper amount of light, warmth, and air-borne water vapor.

LIGHT

The easiest way to tell if your plants are getting the right amount of light is to watch them for tell-tale signs. If they are full of blossoms and the foliage is a good color, they must be getting as much as they need. If the leaves grow rank and long-stemmed and do not have many flowers, the plant is starved for light. If the leaves bleach out paler than they should be and try to curl down around the pot, the plant is getting too much.

Drooping leaves show too much light; rank stems indicate too little light

Unfortunately, the degree of light that will produce the most blooms does not grow the finest foliage; so, in order to have moderately good-looking leaves and still get a fair allowance of flowers, you will have to compromise a little.

It is not true that a violet must never have any sunlight. Sunlight is good for it in moderate amounts. Plants grow beautifully in a north window in summertime, but may not bloom very freely in winter. An east window with a roof overhang is probably the best location. Many people grow them successfully in south and west windows. In that case some means of protection from strong sunlight must be provided. If the window is not screened by trees, shrubs, or vines outside, the light must be controlled by venetian blinds, bamboo blinds, plastic screen or glass curtains. Venetian blinds are excellent if you remember to adjust them as the light changes. Some people have found translucent plastic sheeting to give good control. I keep my plants in south and west windows and protect them with three thicknesses of glass curtains.

Not all of the light that enters your windows comes directly from the sun and the sky. Some of it is reflected off flat surfaces nearby. If your house is surrounded with green lawns, trees, and shrubbery, you do not have to worry too much about reflection, because the light will be softened by the vegetation. But you may have to take protective measures if your windows are exposed to a paved driveway, a white wall or light-colored roof, or if you are near a body of water such as a lake or the ocean, or if you are next to a stretch of sandy beach. Light reflected from an expanse of snow is often too intense for violets.

Another, and much simpler, method of calculating the intensity of light is recommended by some successful growers. Hold your hand about four inches above the plants. If you can see a very faint shadow cast on the leaves, the light is adequate.

In addition to the intensity of the light, the period of its duration is vital to proper growth. During the summer, of course, there is no need to worry about the length of the light day. But in the short, dark days of winter, the period of exposure is often too short. Experiments conducted by the University of California have indicated that a 12-hour exposure of light per day is best for producing maximum bloom. The only way to approach this requirement in winter is to lengthen the day by using electric lights.

In recent years, mobile carts and racks with lights have become very popular. This equipment is advertised in many of the flower magazines. The carts are available in several sizes, and are lighted by fluorescent tubes. They enable you to grow plants in almost any corner of the house. You will find it an added convenience to have the lights connected to an automatic timer, which will turn them on and off at the proper times if you forget or are away from home.

Some correspondents report excellent results with fluorescent lighting. Mrs. Bertha Human writes that she has two 40-watt tubes hung 18 inches from above the soil. Tested with a photoelectric meter, the light has the same intensity as at her north window. With a daily exposure of 12 hours, the plants grow and flower beautifully. She writes that the coloring is dark, lush, and very glossy. The plants appear to suffer no shock when transferred to a window site.

Another correspondent, Mrs. Ferne Kellar, also reports success with an 80-watt fluorescent fixture. She keeps the lights 15 inches above the tops of the pots. She has found this height produces the best flowers. Above 15 inches, the plants yielded plenty of leaves but no blooms. On a 12-hour daily exposure, her plants produce darker foliage and larger flowers than when grown in a window.

Many commercial growers favor fluorescent lights. One well-known eastern grower uses two 40-watt tubes, 8 inches from the top of the plant, turned on 14 to 16 hours per day. However, there are others who claim that their best results come from using the lights 12 hours per day, with humidity 60 per cent, temperature 65 degrees to 70 degrees, and the lights suspended 11 inches above the top of the pots.

The best arrangement is to pair one warm white and one cool white tube. Put the plants with dark foliage under the center of the lights, and the plants with light foliage at the edges where the light is not so intense. Plants with girl foliage do better at the edges in the lower light intensity.

If your plants are getting too much light they will show it by bleached or browned leaves, tight centers, misshapen leaves, or leaves curled down over the edge of the pot. On the other hand, if the light is not strong enough the leaves will grow very upright and "long legged," and there will be few blossoms.

Under fluorescent lights the plants grow twice as rapidly and bloom in half the time as those grown solely in daylight. The leaves are lush and much darker in color. The blue flowers are bluer, but the reds are usually not quite so red. Other colors do not seem to be affected. After coming into bloom, the plants may be removed and put in a window with no change in blooming *provided* that the temperature and humidity are the same. If they drop their flowers when moved it is usually because of a change in temperature and humidity.

One little item that may interest you is that spoon-leaved varieties seem to "spoon" better in very strong light and a rather dry atmosphere than in other conditions. Some of my pet spoon-leaved varieties will spoon beautifully in my window where the light is very strong and the air is very dry, but when the same plants are placed in a greenhouse, they hardly spoon at all.

Not all violets respond the same to fluorescent lighting. Some of them do not do so well; indeed, a few varieties burn. Before investing in an expensive fluorescent installation, therefore, you would be wise to experiment on a small scale and with plants that are not in your priceless category.

TEMPERATURE

The question of the proper temperature for growing African violets is a subject of much argument. Although it is true that the violet is a tropical plant that does not like cold weather and strong drafts, it will not thrive under hothouse conditions either.

African violets will survive extremes of temperature with surprising hardiness. They have been known to grow fairly well in temperatures that go down to freezing at night. I know of a collection that survived in an unheated garage during weather that froze ice in the yard outside, but they did not bloom. Of course, they had become accustomed to the cold by degrees as the winter advanced. Had they been moved from the house to the garage in the dead of winter, their fate would probably have been different.

I know of a nurseryman who keeps his greenhouses heated to about 80 degrees. His violets grow very rapidly, develop long lanky stems, and bloom when quite young. But when transferred to a living room, these plants take from six months to a year to bloom again, and most of their old tops die off.

Some of the most successful growers keep their greenhouse temperatures at 65 degrees both day and night. Not long ago the University of California conducted a long series of experiments with African violets under controlled conditions. Their conclusions indicated that the best results were obtained with temperatures ranging from 57 to 63 degrees during 12 hours of light and from 68 to 73 degrees during the dark period. But, of course, this was all done under controlled conditions. In our homes we do not have such control. For house culture, a daytime temperature of 70 degrees and a night temperature of 60 degrees has proved very satisfactory.

A sudden change in temperature will often give the plants a setback that will take some time to overcome. I notice that whenever the temperature reading in my house goes above 80 degrees, all the flowers will fall off within a few minutes. With some varieties, a change from one window to another will have the same effect. So will watering with water that is cooler than the room.

HUMIDITY

The amount of water-vapor in the atmosphere has a decided effect on violets. The plants will live and grow nice foliage in a too-dry atmosphere, but they will not bloom.

In their native habitat, the violets are accustomed to humidity running from 60 to 70 per cent. We would find such an atmosphere impossible to maintain in our homes—and impossible to live with as well. In many localities, homes average only 10 to 25 per cent humidity, which is too dry for both humans and plants—45 to 50 per cent is ideal.

As it would be oppressive to keep our homes at 60 to 70 per cent humidity just to coddle our violets, the best we can do for them is to provide them with a moist atmosphere all their own. There are several ways of doing this.

In very dry houses, you may stand the potted plants on a couple of inches of wet sand in a tray or shallow box. When I first started growing violets, my plants stubbornly refused to bloom until I figured out a way to arrange a sand box and give them the humidity they needed. I used chick feeders for this purpose. If you are interested in converting them yourself, here is the method.

Obtain from a poultry supply house the chick feeding tray recommended for half-grown chicks. These are about 4 inches deep, 5 or 6 inches wide, and come in various lengths. Buy a length that will fit your window sill. Remove the wire guards that keep the chicks from climbing into the food, seal the joints with solder, and paint the inside with asphalt paint. Paint the outside to suit your decorative fancy, and fill the box with 2 inches of sand.

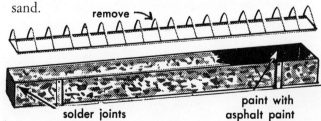

remove →

solder joints   paint with asphalt paint

Lois B. Hammond

GORGEOUS

Lois B. Hammond

WHITE BEAUTY

Of course, if you prefer, you can buy a window sill box ready-made from garden supply stores or you can have one made to order by a sheet metal shop.

To use a sandbox, set a row of potted plants on the sand. Keep the sand very moist but not so damp that puddles form on the surface. The sand is not to be kept wet for watering the plants, but simply for giving off moisture by evaporation. Whenever you add water, pour it on hot, as the steam will be very good for the plants. Once every six weeks add a little nicotine insecticide or household bleach to the water to discourage pests and algae.

I keep all my pots in trays containing about an inch of coarse, moist vermiculite. When the atmosphere gets too dry I use a portable electric humidifier, available in most drug stores, and in especially dry weather, I run it from four to six hours a day.

The type of heat you have in your house may affect your plants. If you have a complete air-conditioning system, or water-cooling system, you do not need to worry too much about your violets. If your home is heated with a floor furnace or a steam radiator, keep an open kettle or a pan of water on it at all times.

Spraying the plants with warm water in a mist sprayer is helpful on dry days. An ordinary fly sprayer is satisfactory for this purpose. Try to get the spray on the underside of the leaves. Do not over-spray. Just a thin mist, like that on a window pane on a cold morning, produces the best results.

Violets like steam. One of the reasons that they often grow better in the kitchen than in any other room is because they thrive on the steam from cooking and dishwashing. Many a plant bought to grace the living room has ended up blooming away in the kitchen for this reason. Bathrooms often provide the right conditions for growing violets successfully.

VENTILATION

If you are one of those people who feels that he must have all the doors and windows open day and night regardless of the weather, you had better grow ivy. Violets cannot stand cold drafts.

Because violets do not like drafts is no reason for believing that they will grow without any ventilation. They must have some fresh air, but not blowing directly on them from an open window or door. Unless there is a fairly good circulation of air, the plants will suffer from mildew or crown rot.

If you live in a locality where the atmosphere is hot and damp, especially in summer, you will have to worry about crown rot. Put the plants in the coolest place you can find where the air can circulate freely. Under trees or on a shady porch, especially on the north side of the house, is a good place. If they are protected from winds and insects, they can be left outside under a tree for the summer.

How to Grow Your Own Seeds

The day will surely come when you will want to try your hand at growing your own seed. You will find it a fascinating operation; but to succeed in such a venture, you will need to know some of the simple facts about the saintpaulia's pollinating habits.

In its natural state, the violet is assisted in the process by visiting insects that scatter pollen; but in your beeless living room, you will have to take over the insects' job and pollinate each flower by hand. In one way, this will give you an advantage over the natural processes — instead of depending on the random ministrations of an insect, you can control the pollinating and produce seed for plants that will have the characteristics that you admire. A chapter a little later on tells how to cross-breed and hybridize violets.

PARTS OF THE FLOWER

Here are the parts of the flower that are involved in producing seed:

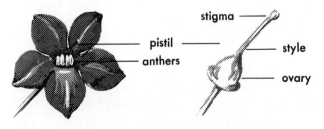

The two little yellow sacs, or *anthers,* in the middle of the flower contain the pollen, which is a dust-like powder. The anthers drop off the plant with the flower when it falls. The tiny horn that looks like a butterfly's feeler is known as the *pistil.*

It remains on the stem when the flower falls. As you can see by the drawing the pistil has three parts. The tip, known as the *stigma,* is connected by the *style* to the *ovary,* which will become the seed pod when fertilized.

When the flower falls off, both the pollen and the stigma are usually ripe for fertilization. The stigma becomes slightly sticky so the pollen will adhere to it. One grain of pollen is enough to fertilize a stigma if both are in the right condition.

Without help from an insect or your own fingers, the pollen may never reach the sticky stigma. Once in a while, the anthers will burst and start shedding pollen before the flower falls off, but as a general rule, the little sacs have to be opened. Sometimes, too, the flower may fall before either the pollen or the stigma is ripe.

HOW TO POLLINATE

To produce seeds for the same variety, you may pollinate the stigma with pollen from the same plant or from another plant of the same variety. To produce seed for a cross, you would use pollen from a plant belonging to a different variety.

The best time for pollinating is the middle of the day when the air is warm. There are several ways to transfer the pollen to the stigma, but most of them are rather fussy. Here is a simple way to go about it:

Take an anther from a fallen flower and open the sac with a needle or clip off a tiny piece with a pair of nail scissors. Pinch the sac a little to spread the opening wider, and apply the opening to the gummy stigma. You can usually see whether any of the pollen adheres or not. To make doubly certain, save the pollen sac and apply it to the same stigma two more times on successive days.

Many people do not know that pollen will keep for at least three months, possibly longer, if it is dried well and kept in a dry, tightly corked vial. In fact, I have successfully pollinated a plant with an anther that was mailed a long distance and then kept a couple of months before I had an opportunity to use it. So if the plant from which you wish to use pollen blossoms ahead of the plant that you want to pollinate, dry the anther well and keep it until you are ready to use it.

After you have pollinated the stigma, you can just sit back and relax. As a rule, the seed pod will begin to develop by the end of a week. You can usually see the pod starting to grow at the end of the calyx.

Successive stages in growth of seed pod

Now you have a long wait before you can see anything else happen. The seed pod grows very slowly, and after it reaches full size, it just sits there week after week. But of course there is plenty of activity inside, even though it is invisible. While the seeds are developing, the stem will often turn at an angle, sometimes almost tying itself into a knot.

When the stem and seed pod turn brown and start to shrivel, the seeds are ripe. The pod usually ripens in about seven months. If pollinated in the early spring, it may ripen in five and a half months; if pollinated in the fall, it may take as long as nine months. Occasionally, an apparently healthy seed pod will turn brown and drop off long before you think it should. Do not throw it away, for it may contain some fertile seeds. Save it and plant the seeds anyway.

When the pod is ripe, pinch it off and put it in an open dish to dry. Set the dish in a warm, bright location, like a window sill. Do not cover. Just how long the pods should be left to dry is one of those differences of opinion that makes African violet culture interesting. Some very successful growers say that the pod should dry for a month before planting. Others, equally successful, say that a week is sufficient.

After the pods have dried out to your satisfaction, break them open and release the powdery seeds. If you are not ready to sow the seeds, you can keep them for several months in a tightly stopped bottle or in small glassine envelopes. If you use a bottle be sure that it is sterile and dry before putting seeds in it. If the seeds get damp and mildewed, they will not grow.

A number of people are now testing a short-term method of ripening violet seed. This is how it is done: record the date of pollinating the flower, and after six weeks have elapsed, cut off the seed pod, leaving a stem on it, and put it in a dry warm place, preferably in the sun, to dry. I pin it on the window curtain. After it has dried six more weeks, open the pod and plant the seeds.

Many people think that when a plant is growing seed pods it should not be allowed to bloom; but one of the most successful breeders I know allows his plants to bloom continuously while they are hanging full of pods in all stages of growth, and he assures me that this has had no effect on the seed-producing capacities of his plants.

CHAPTER ELEVEN

Cross-Breeding and Hybridizing

If you have an experimental turn of mind and would like to try your hand at developing a new variety of saintpaulia or improving an existing one, you will probably find yourself sooner or later involved in a cross-breeding project.

Cross-breeding is a method of pollinating under controlled conditions to transfer certain desired qualities in a plant, such as a particular color, a specific type of leaf, or some other characteristic. To accomplish this, pollen is transferred from the flower of one variety to the stigma of another variety. The seedlings that result from this cross-pollination are allowed to mature, and they in turn may be cross-pollinated among themselves and with their parents. This procedure may be repeated for several successive plant generations until the desired combinations of qualities are obtained.

Traits are passed from one generation to the next in a very intricate pattern. When plants are cross-bred the resulting seeds carry a mixture of the traits of both parent plants. To what exact degree these traits will appear in the offspring depends on several factors. Nature locks a whole complex of traits into the tiny seeds: some, known as "dominants," will be expressed in the offspring more often than other traits known as "recessives." Some of the transmitted traits, such as blossom color and leaf shape, will be obvious enough for the amateur breeder to recognize in the offspring but others will be so subtle — delicate changes in leaf veining, stem formation, or growing habits — that only a trained and experienced geneticist could detect them. Thus, a plant grown from cross-pollinated

seed may appear to be identical to one of the parents when it is actually different in many minute but significant ways.

When two species (such as Ionantha and Kewensis) are cross-pollinated, the offspring are likely to resemble the parent plant that has the greater number of dominant traits. Actually, of course, the offspring may only appear to resemble the parent, because painstaking comparison would probably show a number of fine differences. But when the offspring are cross-bred in their turn — that's when the fun begins. Each of the offspring will contain a highly complex pattern of dominant and recessive traits inherited from both parents, and when this mixture is itself mixed, almost anything can result. Most African violet varieties are at this stage now. They are the product of a long chain of crossing and re-crossing, and any further crossing is likely to produce most interesting and often unexpected results.

As you can probably gather, cross-breeding is likely to provide you with plenty of surprises, because you often have no way of knowing what recessive traits are carried by the parent plants, waiting to be expressed in the progeny. In breeding for color, for instance, you cannot blend your colors as you would paint. If you crossed a red flower with a white one to produce a plant with rose-pink blossoms, you might get pink blooms but you might also get purple, white, red, or some other color. To work toward pink blossoms, you might have to grow several generations before you got the desired color.

Lois B. Hammond

SILVER CLOUD *used in arrangement*

Orchard Nursery

SUNSET LANE

Orchard Nursery

DUPONT LAVENDER

Lois B. Hammond

DOLLY DIMPLES

GOALS IN CROSS-BREEDING

Usually, a person starts on a series of breeding experiments with a definite goal in mind. Cross-breeding may be attempted to bring out recessive forms and colors. In breeding violets, bear in mind that blue is dominant over all other colors and pink is dominant over white. The plain leaf of the Blue Boy type is the dominant leaf form, and even in a cross of two Girl-type plants the plain leaf will be dominant.

At its simplest level, cross-breeding may be attempted between two plants in an effort to combine the best features of both in a new plant. For example, you might have a plant with handsome foliage but ordinary blossoms which you would like to cross with another plant that has better blooms, in the hope of producing a new plant that will have both attractive foliage and colorful blossoms.

For the advanced experimenter, there are a number of marks at which to aim. There is not a true red, such as we see in the gloxinia which belongs to the same family. The orchid varieties could stand a good deal of improvement in color; and some of the whites and pinks have poor foliage. The doubles could be greatly improved. Many breeders are working night and day to produce the unattainable yellow.

Some of the improvements we need now are:

Plants that really come 100 per cent true from leaf cuttings, and stay true.

Singles that will not drop their blossoms for at least a week after opening.

Plants of strong and vigorous growth, that do not need coddling, and that are resistant to rots, mold, and mildew.

Varieties that grow naturally to a symmetrical form without too much training, that have stems stiff enough to hold up the leaves, and flowers carried well above the leaves.

We have a few varieties that will produce two flower stems to each leaf. We need more like that, and ones that will have five, six, or more flowers to a stem, instead of merely two or three.

We also need doubles that will really open, and not stay half-closed and gnarly looking.

HOW TO GO ABOUT IT

If you are seriously interested in attempting an experiment in cross-breeding African violets, you should plan to conduct the project systematically and you should expect to devote several years and possibly a good deal of your shelf space to it. Here are a few basic points to keep in mind:

1. Pollinate the plants exactly as recommended in the chapter on growing your own seed.

2. If your cross-pollinated plant sets a seed pod, label the plant with a little plastic tag showing the two variety names and the date, as "Blue Girl X White King, 2/15/51." It is customary to write the name of the seed parent first. Hang the tag on the stem with a loop of thread.

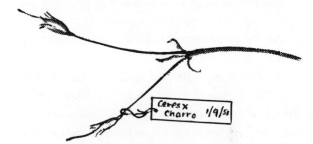

Identify cross-pollinated pods with tag

3. When the seeds are ready for sowing, be sure to sow enough of them to produce a large quantity of seedlings. Some experimenters work with too few plants to obtain the maximum number of recombinations.

4. Keep a careful record of every step in the process. Record the parents' names and date of pollinization; and when the seedlings appear, record full data about their appearance, their rate of growth, etc. Note when they first bloom and record the colors of bloom, size, shape, etc. When you cross each new generation, record all pertinent information about each individual cross.

5. If you obtain a plant which seems to be an improvement on an old one, it may be propagated vegetatively and introduced as a new variety.

6. Cross-breeding is a fascinating but complicated operation. If you are in earnest about your experiments, you will be wise to read up on the subject. Ask your reference librarian for some painless books on plant genetics.

Many amateur hybridizers apparently do not know that they should not stop with the first cross between two selected parents. Even better results may possibly be produced by crossing two of the seedlings with each other, and you should also cross one of the seedlings back to each parent. You can use the same seedling with both parents if you do not want to keep so many seedlings.

REGISTERING NEW VARIETIES

If you produce a plant that seems to you to be a new variety or an improvement on some existing variety, it may be propagated from leaf cuttings to build up a stock for introduction.

It should be registered with the African Violet Society of America. Write to the Committee on Registration, in care of the *African Violet Magazine,* and ask for blank forms for registration. When they arrive, fill them out, and return them to the committee chairman.

Your application will be published in the *African Violet Magazine,* and if it is not contested, the registration will become permanent. It can be contested on several grounds. The name may have been used by someone else, another grower may claim a prior right to the name, or someone else may claim to have produced the same variety before you did. In case of any objection to the registration, the question is decided by the committee.

HYBRIDIZING WITH PLANTS IN SAME FAMILY

The African violet belongs to the gesneria family, and has a number of cousins, some of them very beautiful, and a cross might produce something very lovely in the way of a hybrid.

Episcias and naegelias have some of the most gorgeously colored leaves in the entire gesneria family, and a cross between either and the violet should produce wonderful foliage. Also, at least two of the naegelias have yellow flowers, and might possibly be the source of the unattainable yellow violet, if such a cross were fertile.

The best-known cousins are gloxinias with their blazing red blossoms — another color which every violet fancier would like to produce. So far, I have been able to cross them only one way successfully. Gloxinias will produce fertile seed if crossed with violet pollen. I grew about 40 plants from such a cross, but of course they all turned out to be gloxinias. I also tried 26 crosses with gloxinia pollen on violet plants, and though 22 pods grew and ripened, not one seed ever germinated.

Persons who have tried to back-cross gloxinias with violets say that they are sterile. One correspondent writes that his crosses of gloxinias and saintpaulias produced some plants of a modified saintpaulia type in a ratio of about one saintpaulia to eight gloxinias, but the plants of the saintpaulia type were weaklings. Only one survived, and it did not bloom.

CHAPTER TWELVE

Variations and Variegation

Anyone who grows violets for any length of time or in any quantity is bound to be surprised occasionally by some unexpected development in his collection of plants. For no apparent reason, a pet plant may some day begin to show spoon-shaped leaves, little rosettes on the stems, variegated leaves or blossoms, or some other change from the norm.

The more highly developed a plant becomes, the more likely it is to produce an occasional departure from the recognized type. Such a departure is known as either a "sport" or a "mutation." The difference between them is that the mutation will breed true from seeds, but the sport will not and must be propagated by cuttings. Sports are becoming increasingly common among the African violets. In fact, one student of the subject has estimated that from every hundred violet leaves put down for propagation at least one sport will be produced. Some of the finest saintpaulia varieties have originated in this manner.

Sometimes sports will not always propagate true. I have in mind a particular variety which is very handsome when it breeds true, but only one plant out of three will do so. If you do propagate what seems to you to be a new variety, you should grow it for two or three generations to make sure that it will "stay put." If you succeed in creating a new variety, register it with the African Violet Society of America.

One authority contends that a sport is more likely to reproduce its own peculiarities if all the stem is trimmed off the leaf before it is set in sand or water.

If the stem is left attached, the leaf is more likely to reproduce the characteristics of the variety.

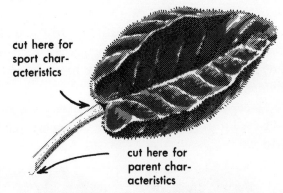

cut here for sport characteristics

cut here for parent characteristics

Control characteristics by cutting stem

TYPES OF SPORTS

The so-called hanging-basket type is a very good example of the peculiarities of sports. It is not a variety by itself, but may occur in any variety. It sends out flower stems with a tuft of leaves between the blossoms; and if the long stem is left on the plant after the flower fades, the plant will usually send out another blossom stalk from the leaf tuft, making the stem look very much like a strawberry

Hanging-basket type African violet

runner. These long stems and tufts hang down over the side of the pot, hence the name a "hanging basket." The leaves of these plants will seldom produce another basket plant, but if the tufts themselves are cut off and rooted, they will quite often breed true.

Spooned leaves are another example of a sport development. They cannot always be depended on to stay spooned. The only spooned plant that can be relied upon is Gorgeous. Any number of the others will spoon beautifully for a while, perhaps for months and years, and then suddenly take to growing flat leaves. I once had a fine large Mentor Boy which was beautifully spooned for about a year, then it suddenly grew all flat leaves and never again produced a spooned leaf. As it had stood in the same place throughout and had not been re-potted, the change could not have been caused by different soil or light.

Some varieties, especially Trilby, have a tendency to grow little rosettes on the leaves or on the stems, like this:

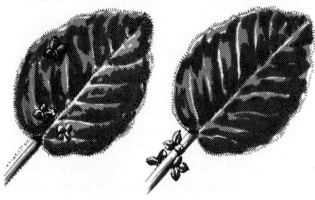

These should be left on until either the leaf dies or they drop off, when they can be set on damp sand or vermiculite and rooted. But they will not necessarily produce plants with the same peculiarity.

CHEMICALLY-PRODUCED MUTATIONS

We do not need to leave the production of mutations entirely to nature. It is possible to hasten the process by the use of chemicals. There are several that are known to have the power to rearrange the chromosomes, but the only one that is at present practical for amateur experiments is colchicine, which is now being used by quite a number of people. It is sold commercially in kits ready for use, with full directions enclosed. These kits contain, besides some unnecessary articles, a jar of ointment and a bottle of 0.2% solution. (Note: Colchicine is a poison and should be handled with extreme care. Do not store it within reach of children.)

Presumably, all the plants that survive treatment with this chemical will be changed in some way. Many of these changes can be discerned only by a microscopic study of the cells, but from 30 to 40 per cent of the plants will show differences clearly visible to the ordinary observer.

Sometimes this change will take the form of curly or wavy leaves, but the most common result will be a supreme form of the original variety. However, even if you get a dozen sprouts from treated leaves of any one variety, there will probably be a variation in leaf form or texture. One of the first signs that you have succeeded in producing a mutation will be the growth of odd-shaped leaves.

These treated plants and leaves grow very slowly and should not be separated until they are quite good-sized, as they die very easily when young. After they get partly grown they are just as healthy as any other plant. Also, if you root a leaf from one of the treated plants it will produce plants which will grow just as fast as any other cutting.

How to Apply Colchicine

There are several methods of applying colchicine, but the following are the most generally preferred. It is also possible to treat seeds, but many who have tried it report that it is not very satisfactory.

1. Application to center bud. Take off the row of leaves just below the center bud, and wrap the stem over the raw spots with a length of narrow cotton tape or loosely twisted string. Be sure the raw spots where the leaves were removed are covered, but do not cover the bud. Put the lower end of the tape in a small bottle of solution, and leave the whole set-up for about a week, watching to see that the bottle does not become empty. Then

Orchard Nursery

GIRLIWINKLE

Orchard Nursery

SNOW PRINCE

Lois B. Hammond

PATRICE

Orchard Nursery

DAD'S BEST GIRL

remove the bottle and tape. For this treatment do not use the solution full strength, use it with an equal amount of water added. For this experiment use well-established small plants, about 3-inch pot size.

The plant will probably try to send out side shoots instead of growing from the tip. Keep them picked off to force tip growth.

2. Immersion. Take several seedlings with four or five leaves, wrap the roots in moist cotton, and cover this with a strip of metal foil to keep the roots moist. Put this bundle of plants tops down in a small glass or short, wide-mouthed bottle partly filled with solution. If using a bottle, make the root-wrapping large enough around to serve as a cork. If a glass is used, suspend the bundle from a small stick rested across the top of the glass. The growing tips should not touch the bottom, but must be kept in the solution.

The leaves should be kept immersed for one to seven days. Take them out every day and look at them. If they begin to look water-soaked, remove from solution and plant at once.

Less than 24 hours in solution does not usually have any effect, and more than a week will kill the plants. The solution I have found best for this treatment is one part of the stock solution (0.2%) to nine parts water.

3. Another treatment is to put a collar of dry cotton and foil around the base of the stems just above the roots, and submerge the roots in the solution instead of the tops. In this case wash all the solution off the roots before planting in soil.

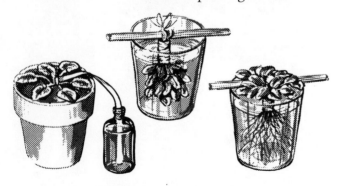

Three ways to apply colchicine solution

The treated plants should be kept in a warm place after planting, out of the sun and under glass or plastic covers until they show signs of growth.

4. Most people prefer to work with individual leaves. One well-known grower first roots leaves in a nutrient solution, one-quarter the usual strength. When the roots are about half an inch long, he takes them out of the solution and lets them dry for an hour or so, then paints the stem just above the roots with colchicine ointment and plants them in his favorite rooting mixture.

5. Another grower takes a leaf with half-inch roots and plants it about half an inch deep in vermiculite. He then takes a dropper full of the 0.2% solution, and lets it run down the stem, being sure that the stem is wet all the way around, not just on one side.

I have better results by first rooting leaves in plain water and removing them from the water just before the new shoots are about to sprout, and then putting them for a week in a solution of 1 part of the 0.2% solution and 9 parts of water before planting in vermiculite.

Leaves under treatment should be kept warm, out of the sun, and under glass or plastic until they start to grow. Never let them get dry. Colchicine treatments are a shock to the plant, and a large percentage of the leaves treated will die.

VARIEGATION

Very little seems to be known about what causes variegation. It must be remembered that when violets were first discovered in Africa, some variegated specimens were found among them, which were classified as saintpaulia variegata.

A few growers hold a theory that variegation is caused by a disease. However, in cases where variegation in other species is caused by a disease, such as mosaic, the disease and markings spread to all nearby plants and the markings reappear in the offspring. But as anyone who has grown African violets knows, the condition never spreads from one plant to another and it is rarely transmitted to the offspring. In addition, when an appearance of variegation is caused by bleaching or sickness, the off-color areas blend gradually into the natural color of the leaves, instead of being sharply defined as in true variegation. If you look at a variegated African violet you will notice that the colored areas are indeed quite clearly defined. There is no more reason to suppose that a variegated violet is sick or diseased than to suppose that a variegated ivy or geranium is diseased.

It is possible to breed variegated African violets at home, but it is a slow and unpredictable task, as I can report from personal experience.

From about fifty leaves taken from my own pet variegated plant, one leaf grew albino plants, which did not live long, one grew a beautifully marked plant just like the parent, and all the rest reverted to plain green.

Some variegated plants never bloom. Others bloom but have small insignificant blossoms. A few bloom normally, and some grow variegated flowers. On the whole, unless your plant is a very large and strong one, it is better to keep the buds picked off, as they tend to weaken the plant.

If some all-green leaves appear on a variegated plant, leave them on, as they will give it strength; but if any green suckers or side branches attempt to come out, pick them off at once. They would soon grow so much stronger than the rest of the plant that they would cause the variegated part to dwindle away.

If the whole plant turns solid green, as many of them do eventually, do not throw it away. It may at any time start sending up variegated leaves again. Some do and some don't. But leaves from it may produce variegated plants at any time.

If you are breeding for variegated leaves, remember that you *must* use a plant with variegated leaves for the seed parent.

When starting plants from leaves, if your leaf sends up a variegated plant, allow the parent leaf to remain attached until it dies for it will give the variegated shoot strength. Do not separate the plants until it is absolutely necessary, as they do not stand repotting as well as other types. If, as usually happens, one or more all-green sprouts come up at the same time, remove them as soon as possible. They will grow faster than the variegated sprouts and will crowd them out.

One reasonably sure way to propagate variegated plants is to nip the center out of your prettiest one and thus force it to grow side shoots. Some of these will be like the parent and can be removed and rooted when they have grown large enough. But of course this will spoil the appearance of the parent plant.

Variegated Plants from the Nursery

The foregoing applies to all variegated plants which appear from leaves of plain green plants, or to plants which for no apparent reason suddenly begin to grow variegated leaves. But in recent years, commercial growers have originated a number of variegated plants which will usually propagate true from leaves. These do not require any special treatment except that they should be given the strongest possible light, short of burning the leaves, and they should receive a fertilizer with a low nitrogen percentage, such as 0-10-10.

If not in strong light, the leaves are apt to turn green. The leaves already grown will not change, but the new leaves just coming out will be solid green. Putting the plant in strong light will cause the new leaves to come out variegated. In very hot weather the plant will often produce all-green leaves, but as soon as the weather cools off, the new leaves will usually begin to come out variegated again.

ALBINO PLANTS

Albino plants are those in which no clear green appears in any of the leaves, although there may be some faint traces of green. They are usually a lovely cream color, and the young leaves often show tints of rose-pink, especially on the edges and along the veins.

They are delicate and difficult to grow. They have a tendency to either die young or turn green.

Lois B. Hammond

PANSY

Robert Cox

DuPont Blue Hybrid

This is because they do not have sufficient chlorophyll in the leaves to manufacture the sugar necessary to maintain them in growing condition.

This difficulty can be corrected to some extent by spraying them with a sugar solution. Ask your druggist to put up the following:

    1 pint distilled water
    1½ ounces granulated sugar
    2 grams sulfanilamide

Before you use it, add a tablespoon of soapy water for a spreader. Keep it in a glass jug or bottle in a cool place, but not in the refrigerator. Apply it with atomizer or fly sprayer one to three times a

week. Spray both the upper and under sides of the leaves and do not put on so much that the leaves drip — they should be just misted over. As this spray is sticky, you had better stand the plant in the sink when you treat it. The leaves will become very dusty during the course of this treatment, so the plant should be washed whenever it begins to look gummy. One authority recommends spraying three times a week, but I find that my plants do well with one spraying a week. This treatment can only be effective in a temperature of about 70 degrees; so do not let your plant stand in a cold place, or the spraying will not have any effect.

CHAPTER THIRTEEN

Controlling Pests and Diseases

As house plants go, the African violet is a fairly hardy type, but it does have its ailments and it is a popular refuge for a few choice pests. Fortunately, you can protect your violet from most pests and diseases, and if they do take hold, you have a good chance of curing the ailment or disposing of the pest.

GENERAL HOUSEKEEPING PRACTICES

If you follow a few simple precautions in handling your plants, you can reduce the possibility of their becoming infected or invaded. In the first place, you should isolate all newly acquired plants for at least a month unless you know positively that they were properly disinfected beforehand. This applies to plants acquired from dealers or friends. If you trade plants with a friend, some of her plants may harbor a disease or insect whose presence she had not noticed. Of course, if your own plants are treated periodically they are not likely to be susceptible to infection.

After handling a diseased or suspected plant, you should always wash your hands with soap and water, and also wash everything that has touched the plant. If you ordinarily use a watering can, do not use it to water the diseased plants, as it may carry infection.

If cut flowers are brought in from outside, do not set them near the violets, as they may carry insects or diseases. Put them at least 6 feet from your violets.

A NOTE ON INSECTICIDES

A word of caution is in order regarding insecticides. Some of the formulas now marketed for home use contain chemicals that are toxic to humans as well as to the pests they control. It is prudent to use them with caution, particularly indoors, where vapors or dusts may stay in the air for a time because of lack of circulation. You should follow label directions exactly, avoiding contact as far as possible with sprays or dusts. Keep bottles, dusters, and sprayers out of children's reach. Remove pets from the room where the plants are to be sprayed, or take the plants to another room. See that there is no uncovered food in the room. After applying the insecticide, wash your hands thoroughly with soap and water.

CYCLAMEN MITE

The most dreaded of all the insects that attack African violets is the cyclamen mite. This insect is too small to be seen without a magnifying glass, but it can be spotted by the damage it does to the plant.

The center is the first to show it. It grows puckered and fuzzy-looking, and usually turns a brownish color or sometimes a light gray as though it had been powdered over with ashes. The stems are shorter than normal and both leaves and stems become very brittle. Small leaves remain undersized and become gnarled and twisted or one-sided and ill-shaped. The buds drop off and any flowers surviving long enough to open are distorted and imperfect.

The best thing to do about cyclamen mite is to prevent it; but if the pest attacks a plant that you just can't bear to part with, you can often save it with proper treatment. After battling mites for over ten years I have adopted a routine procedure which I follow when I discover an infested plant. First, I take off five or six leaves from the plant, not from the top or center, but from about the second or third row from the bottom. From each leaf, I cut off all the stem but about an inch, dip the leaves three times in a good insecticide, letting them dry after each dip, and set them to root.

Then I take the rest of the plant, burn it, dispose of the soil, boil or bake the pot and saucer, and wash the shelf with disinfectant. Then I dunk all the rest of the plants in insecticide.

Recently better remedies than sodium selenate have been developed for treating Cyclamen mites in plants. They do not kill the plants or discolor the blossoms, and are not so dangerous to handle as the sodium selenate.

Spray the plants thoroughly with an insecticide containing diazinon or guthion (as directed for indoor plants) letting some of the solution dribble down the stems into the soil. Repeat once a week for at least three weeks, or at the intervals stated on the spray label.

APHIS

Aphis do not ordinarily attack African violets, but in case they get on the leaves, they can be disposed of by spraying the plant with a nicotine sulfate or malathion solution. This must be repeated every week for at least three weeks to catch the new aphis that will hatch out. Aphis on the roots can usually be killed by watering the plant with a solution of nicotine sulfate or malathion, or with a solution made by dissolving a 7½-grain tablet of bichloride of mercury in 1 gallon of water. Repeat a week later. Be sure the soil is dry when you apply this and put it on from the top. A rotenone insecticide may also be used for this purpose.

Sometimes, aphis may be forced off the plant by turning a stream of water through the foliage. They are likely to return, however.

SPRINGTAILS

Springtails are little white insects that thrive in the soil around the plant. Although they do no harm to the plant, they are a nuisance and may be killed by treating the plant as for aphis in the soil.

STUNT

The ravages of stunt look something like those of cyclamen mite. The leaves become thickened and brittle, do not grow to normal size, and usually get lighter in color. The stems are short and thick, and the flowers, if any appear, are misshapen. There is no known cure, so you might as well throw away the plant and grow a new one. As it is difficult to distinguish between stunt and cyclamen mite, treat affected plants for cyclamen mite first. In neither case will the leaves already on the plant ever become normal in appearance; but if the deformity is caused by mite, the new leaves will come in healthy-looking after treatments. If it is stunt, they will not.

NEMATODES

Nematodes are tiny worms that cause knots to form on the roots, and sometimes on the stems. The roots may be so full of knots that they look like strings of beads. The plants slowly starve, become a sickly color, and finally die.

This trouble is soil-borne and can be prevented by sterilizing the potting soil, provided you do not have an infected plant in the group which will infect the others. When you mix a batch of potting soil, sterilize it as a precaution with an organic phosphorous nematocide following label directions. Mix it thoroughly, cover, and let stand at least two weeks before using.

When treating potted plants that are already infected, be sure the soil is moist and drench with the material in concentration as recommended on the label. Soak plants once a week for at least three weeks, and prevent the solution from touching the leaves.

This method will kill nematodes, but not all the other pests that infest potting soils. I recommend that *all* potting mixes, both commercial and home-mixed, be sterilized by baking before use. I bake mine for 2½ hours at 250 degrees. It should be well moistened before putting in to bake. Let stand a couple of days before using.

CROWN ROT

Crown rot is a most common ailment. The first indication is usually the wilting of the lower row of leaves, as if the plant needed water. The causes are many and varied: watering with cold water, keeping the plant too wet, too-heavy soil, poor ventilation, too large a pot for the plant, the crown too deep in the soil, water standing too long in the heart of the plant, or sudden changes of temperature. The usual cause is overwatering.

The most successful treatment is to cut the plant off above the wilted leaves, remove the bottom row of good leaves, and root the top in a glass of water. Do not let the water come up to the remaining leaves; the end of the stem should not be more than half an inch under water. The good leaves you picked off may be rooted in your usual manner.

In some localities where the water supply is treated with chemicals at certain times of the year, the plants may develop a condition similar to crown rot. If the case is not too extreme and the plant is not too badly affected, it can be saved sometimes by watering with a vinegar solution, as recommended for alkali soils. Some growers remove the plant from the pot, wash all the soil off the roots, repot in fresh soil, and water with rainwater or distilled water. If this fails to revive an ailing plant within 24 hours, cut it off and re-root. Usually only a few plants are affected, as some varieties seem to be more resistant than others.

LEAF STEM ROT

Leaf stem rot is distinguished from crown rot by the fact that neither the roots of the plant nor the crown are affected, only the stem of an individual leaf or leaves at the point where the leaf stem is joined at the base to the plant. Sometimes the leaf also has soft brown spots on the surface. The remedy is to pull off the affected leaves and brush the raw surfaces on the stem of the plant with a dry brush dipped in powdered sulfur, or Fermate.

THRIPS

A lot of tiny scars on the under surface of the leaves is a sure sign of thrips. These are tiny insects, barely visible, that look like moving flyspecks. They are generally found on the buds and live and hatch on the under side of the leaves. They also live in the soil and on the pot saucer and shelf.

I have found that the best remedy is to submerge the plant in a mild solution of nicotine sulfate. This must be repeated several times at weekly intervals. Other treatments: dust with rotenone or sulfur dust, or spray with rotenone, nicotine sulfate, or malathion solution. As the insects live on the under side of the leaf, you must make sure that the spray or dust reaches the under surface.

Don't forget to disinfect the pots, saucers, and pot shelf whenever you treat the plant.

RING SPOT

Not too much seems to be known about ring spot. Yellow ring-shaped spots develop on the leaves, and sometimes combine in fantastic patterns. It is thought not to be a disease, but rather to be the effect of too much direct sun, especially on leaves after spraying or overhead watering. The remedy is to cut off some of the sun or remove the plant to a more shaded position.

BUD DROP

Bud drop is a very common complaint. It may be caused by a number of things, and is not a disease of itself. It can be caused by thrips, gas fumes, too-dry air, too-acid soil, too much fertilizer, too much nitrogen in the soil, or an unsuitable soil mixture. About nine times out of ten the cause is lack of humidity in the air. Sometimes sudden, extreme changes in temperature will cause the buds to drop, though usually only opened flowers are affected.

ANTHRACNOSE

Recently there have been reports of anthracnose on violets. The indications are: pin holes in the leaves and round or irregular sunken spots, whitish in color, on the under sides. These spots eventually turn brown around the edges and finally the leaves wilt and die.

There is a treatment for this, but it is complicated and in many cases not very successful. The best cure is to burn the plant and soil and sterilize the pot.

WORMS OR FLIES

Water with a solution of household bleach, two teaspoonfuls to a quart of water. Do not use this on small or newly potted plants.

Or water with a solution of lime water, one teaspoonful to one quart of water.

CURLING LEAVES

Sometimes these are caused by thrips. Look for them on the under sides of leaves, and on flower buds.

It can also be caused by too much light, sudden changes in temperature, especially from warm to cold, and by excessive dryness of the air.

Some varieties will curl their leaves for no reason that anyone can see. It is just their nature.

If the leaves of a normally upright variety curl down over the sides of the pot, and there are no insects on them, and the temperature has not been too cold at any time, the curling may be caused by too much light. Set the plant down on a bottom shelf below the window, and the leaves will usually begin to reach up.

But if the small center leaves turn in to the center at an abrupt angle, or with a twist, suspect mites, and treat as if for mites.

MEALY BUGS

If there are only a few mealy bugs, pick them off with a toothpick and cotton swab, dipped in alcohol. If there are many, spray every week for 5 weeks with a 12 per cent malathion compound, 1 teaspoon to 1 gallon of water.

SOIL MEALY BUGS

We have always had these in the garden, but they have only recently discovered the African violet. They live down in the soil and eat off the fine, hair-like feeding roots. There are varied opinions about the proper treatment of this pest.

Dr. Paul Nelson, of Cornell Research Laboratory, suggests the pot and soil ball be submerged in a solution of malathion for two or three minutes. Use 55 per cent emulsifiable malathion at the rate of 1 tablespoon to 1 gallon of water. Give 3 treatments 10 days apart. Use rubber gloves while dipping and handling pots.

One grower recommends a lawn fungicide containing benzine hexachloride, 4 level tablespoons in 3 gallons of water. Use 3 times at intervals of 10 days. Be sure the soil is damp before using.

A new and much simpler treatment has also been reported to me. Buy napthalene flakes, or if unavailable, pulverize some mothballs. For a 4-inch pot use a small pinch, or a smaller amount for a smaller pot, and put on top of the soil. Water it well. I am told this does not injure the plant, and that a second application is usually not necessary. I recommend keeping a sharp eye on the plant, however, in case not all the eggs were destroyed.

CHAPTER FOURTEEN

Grooming Plants for the Show Room

If you have a fine African violet plant that you would like to enter in a show, you will want to acquaint yourself with the standards by which violets are judged.

In all well-conducted shows, the judges have no personal interest in any of the entries that they examine. They do not know and have no way of knowing to whom a plant belongs, for the owner's name is concealed until after the judges have made their selections. If a judge has entered a plant in the show, he is not permitted to grade the section where his entry is displayed. When possible, judges are invited from another community or at least from another club, so they will have no personal concern with the entries.

Contrary to general impression, the size of the plant and the number of blossoms are not the only characteristics by which a plant is rated. In most shows, the entries are judged for five qualities: symmetry of form, quantity of bloom, cultural condition, size of bloom, and color of bloom. Each of these qualities is assigned a point value, and plants are graded on a point basis.

SYMMETRY OF PLANT (30 POINTS)

Symmetry of leaf pattern or form counts for the highest score in judging. It is the most difficult quality to achieve because it requires long and careful attention to the plant's growth and development.

Aside from the peculiarities of certain varieties with which any experienced judge is well acquainted, there are a few well-known types of growth, such as: the Ionantha types, long-stemmed and tall-grow-

ing; the intermediate, with shorter stems and more rounded habit of growth; the flat or rosette type; the "Girl" type, distinguished by its scalloped leaves and white spot at the base of the leaves; and the large, plushy-leaved DuPonts, Supremes, and Amazons. Also, the dwarfs, which vary in type. There are a few of the "droopy" type, which will curl the leaves down around the pot no matter how they are grown.

To attain a symmetrical leaf pattern, you must begin preparing the plant at the time it is first put into a pot by itself. Set the tiny plant in the exact center of the pot. As it grows, turn the pot around often so the plant will be evenly exposed to light and air and will not grow one-sided. The stem should grow perfectly straight and upright, and the only way to keep it straight is to turn the plant often, at least twice a week, preferably once a day.

The lower row of leaves should be evenly spaced and the other rows should form a symmetrical pattern all the way up the stem. If they persist in growing in such a manner that a gap is left in the circle,

or if a stem gets broken off, the other leaves can be trained to fill the gap in a couple of weeks. Start off by working the leaves part way into position and pegging them in place with toothpicks. Every few days move them a little farther along until they finally close the gap. After a week or so, remove the pegs and the stems will stay in place.

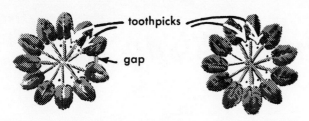

If your plant is a flat rosette type and one leaf sticks up too far, it can be trained to lie down with the rest. Straighten out a wire hairpin, bend a crook in one end and hook it over the leaf stem, and imbed the other end in the dirt. Push the hairpin a little deeper in the pot each day until the leaf lies down where it belongs.

Pick off all damaged and irregularly shaped leaves from your show plants and train others to fill the gaps. If one leaf has too long a stem and sticks out so far that it breaks the pattern, take it off. A medium-sized plant with a good leaf pattern will score over a larger one with an irregular shape.

Never let a sucker or a side shoot grow on your show plant. It will disqualify it for the single-crown class, and if left on will ruin the shape of the plant. Poke or nip it out before it gets big enough to leave a gap or scar.

There is usually a section for multiple-crown plants in each show. If you want to enter multiple-crowns, keep them as well balanced as possible. For instance, if your plant has three crowns, they should be as nearly as possible of equal size and so spaced that they do not crowd each other out of shape. If some of the leaves at the center between the crowns grow too long to look attractive, or try to crowd each other out of shape, take some of them out.

QUANTITY OF BLOOM (25 POINTS)

Quantity of bloom is second in importance. This takes into consideration not only the number of opened flowers, but also the number of buds visible, although some judges do not agree on the matter

of the buds. Other things being equal, judges will sometimes count the blossoms on rival plants in an effort to reach a fair decision. In such a case, the judges have to keep in mind the type and variety of the competing plants, for some varieties are very free bloomers, while others, such as the Amazon, rarely open more than one cluster of blooms at a time.

CULTURAL CONDITION (20 POINTS)

The next in importance is cultural condition. No matter if an entry is as big as a dishpan and has a hundred blossoms, it will not be apt to win a prize if it is dirty, or full of ragged leaves and dead bloom stalks.

The leaves should be healthy looking and evenly colored. None of them should be spotted or scarred, or bleached by too much sun, or turning brown around the edges.

Before taking your plant to the show, be sure that it is free of insects, that the leaves are clean and dustless, and that all dead stems and flowers are removed, not only from the plant but from the soil surface in the pot as well. Some of the plants I have seen entered in shows were so dusty and untidy that they looked as if they had been found in an attic!

SIZE OF BLOOMS (15 POINTS)

Size of blooms is fourth on the list, and this also takes into account the variety, as the Amazons, Du-Ponts and Supremes are supposed to have larger blooms than the others, and most of the dwarfs and miniatures have small flowers.

COLOR OF BLOOMS (10 POINTS)

Color of blooms is considered last of all, mainly because it varies so much by reason of differences in soil, water, and light intensity.

PREPARING YOUR PLANT FOR SHOW

Very few plants score a 100 on this scale; so if your plant is not a perfect specimen, don't be hesitant about entering it anyway.

Orchard Nursery

Orchard Nursery

Plant stands like those shown above effectively display violet collections

Before you take it to the show, don't forget the little and obvious things, such as:

1. Wash the outside of the pot thoroughly.

2. Write the name of the variety on a plant tag and place it where it can be plainly seen, as most people at a show like to know what they are looking at.

3. Write your name in pencil on a piece of adhesive tape and stick it to the bottom of the pot where it will not be visible to the judges or the public. This is for purposes of identification in case of any mix-up. Don't write in ink or indelible pencil, as the writing may blur or disappear in water.

CHAPTER FIFTEEN

Saintpaulia Species

In the last two or three years people have become captivated by species Saintpaulias. If you are interested in plant breeding, these species have great possibilities for you. Some work has been done with them, but not enough.

S. amaniensis is a trailer, and cannot be grown to a single crown. The small, medium-green leaves are almost round, short-stemmed, and inclined to curl. The flowers are single, small, and pale-blue. It has many small branches, is a rather poor bloomer, and needs plenty of water, a cool place, and less light than the hybrid varieties.

S. confusa was first called *kewensis* and later, *diplotricha*. It is now officially called *confusa*. It can be grown to a single crown, but has a decided tendency to bend its neck and grow to one side of the pot; it makes a better-looking plant if allowed to grow about three, evenly-spaced crowns. It has a small, slightly serrated, almost round, grayish-green leaf, and a small, light-blue flower. It can take fairly strong light.

S. difficilis is also known as "Kenya" and "Tanga." Perhaps one reason it has so many names is that there are two and possibly more distinct variations in the species, but the variations are slight, and they are both, or all, *difficilis*. It is a single crown plant of upright growth with rather long stems, and long, distinctly-veined, pointed leaves. The flowers are medium size and medium blue. It is a fairly good bloomer, and can take the same treatment as the regular varieties.

S. diplotricha is also known as "Mkulumuzu." There are at least four slight variations in this species, but they are all *diplotricha*. It is a flat, rosette type with rather thick leaves a little more than an inch long, serrated, slightly pointed, and inclined to spoon. It grows well to a single crown, is fairly small, and seldom outgrows a 3-inch pot. The flowers are small, pale-blue, almost white. It can take strong light, but is a rather poor bloomer.

S. goetzeana is the pincushion type, small-growing, with multiple short branches. It cannot be grown to a single crown. The leaves are small, dark, and oval. The flowers are said to be a lilac color. It has also been said that it will not bloom under cultivation, and, it is, in fact, extremely difficult to keep alive. A cool temperature is required, with subdued light and very high humidity.

S. grandifolia grows upright and rather large, with moderately-long, flexible petioles, and thin-textured, medium-sized, oval leaves. It will grow well to a single crown, produce medium light-blue flowers, bloom fairly well, and take good light. There are at least two variations of this species; one of them has been known as "Lutinde," but they are both *grandifolia*.

S. grotei is generally called a climber, but this is a misnomer. It is a sprawler, and if not grown in a hanging basket or pot, will need to be fastened to a trellis or plant pole for support. Some of the main branches will grow to be three feet long. It cannot be grown to a single crown. A fairly good bloomer, it produces medium-blue, single, long flowers, and has long, flexible petioles and thin leaves. It needs plenty of water and fertilizer and rather subdued light.

S. intermedia grows upright to a single crown. The leaves are olive-green, almost round, finely serrated, and have a tendency to spoon. The flowers are blue single. It is easy to grow with ordinary care.

S. ionantha, one of the first violets cultivated, is the many-times great-grandparent of the majority of the popular varieties now grown. A rather ordinary-looking plant, it is long-stemmed and upright with medium-blue, single flowers. It is a fairly good bloomer and grows naturally to a single crown.

S. magungensis is a trailer which cannot be grown to a single crown. It has creeping brown stems, many short branches, and heart-shaped, small leaves with beautiful veining. The outer row of leaves is apt to bend down at an acute angle. The flowers are medium violet-blue singles with darker centers.

S. nitida is upright in growth, has a single crown, small, medium dark-green, smooth, oval leaves and slender, flexible, brown petioles. The flowers are blue single.

S. orbicularis is of upright growth and does not do well as a single crown. It has rather small, roundish leaves on long, thin, flexible stems. It is a very free bloomer and has small, light-lilac blossoms with dark centers.

S. pendula grows upright to a single crown. Leaves are gray-green, almost round, slightly serrated, flat, and moderately heavy-textured. The flowers are blue single. It does well with ordinary care.

S. shumensis is a midget, multiple-crowned, and of rather flat growth. It has small, almost-round leaves, short petioles, and almost-white flowers. It can take strong light, but is rather sensitive to water.

S. tongwensis grows to a single crown, but has a tendency to grow one-sided and creep to the edge of the pot. It has rather long, moderately-narrow leaves, and pale-blue flowers. One of the variations of this species has a narrow leaf with a pale-green streak down the center. It needs subdued light.

S. velutina is better known as "Coxiensis" or "H C ensis," as it was introduced by the late Harvey Cox. It is a very handsome plant of upright growth, with flexible stems and slightly furry, scalloped, heart-shaped leaves with red backs and stems and pronounced veining. It grows to a single crown, is a free bloomer, and produces small, pale-blue flowers. It needs good light, but is rather sensitive to water.

Index

PHOTOGRAPHERS

We wish to thank the following people for the photographs used in this book:
Lois B. Hammond, Irvington, California
Orchard Nursery, Lafayette, California
Shaffer's Tropical Gardens, Capitola, Calif.